T0158958

No More Fear

Karen T. Stratoti

WestBow
PRESS®
A DIVISION OF THOMAS NELSON
& ZONDERVAN

Copyright © 2017 Karen T. Stratoti.

All rights reserved. No part of this book may be used or reproduced by any means, graphic, electronic, or mechanical, including photocopying, recording, taping or by any information storage retrieval system without the written permission of the author except in the case of brief quotations embodied in critical articles and reviews.

Scripture texts in this work are taken from the New American Bible, revised edition © 2010, 1991, 1986, 1970 Confraternity of Christian Doctrine, Washington, D.C. and are used by permission of the copyright owner. All Rights Reserved. No part of the New American Bible may be reproduced in any form without permission in writing from the copyright owner.

Author Credits: CEO of Excellence in Caring, LLC
Cover design by Edward J. Wright III

This book is a work of non-fiction. Unless otherwise noted, the author and the publisher make no explicit guarantees as to the accuracy of the information contained in this book and in some cases, names of people and places have been altered to protect their privacy.

WestBow Press books may be ordered through booksellers or by contacting:

WestBow Press
A Division of Thomas Nelson & Zondervan
1663 Liberty Drive
Bloomington, IN 47403
www.westbowpress.com
1 (866) 928-1240

Because of the dynamic nature of the Internet, any web addresses or links contained in this book may have changed since publication and may no longer be valid. The views expressed in this work are solely those of the author and do not necessarily reflect the views of the publisher, and the publisher hereby disclaims any responsibility for them.

Any people depicted in stock imagery provided by Thinkstock are models, and such images are being used for illustrative purposes only.
Certain stock imagery © Thinkstock.

ISBN: 978-1-5127-9554-7 (sc)
ISBN: 978-1-5127-9556-1 (hc)
ISBN: 978-1-5127-9555-4 (e)

Library of Congress Control Number: 2017910940

Print information available on the last page.

WestBow Press rev. date: 09/08/2017

Contents

Preface

God uses everything that happens in our life for His purpose.

I have just assisted one of my dearest friends, Dianne, in dealing with her husband's rare metastatic stomach cancer. They have just prepared for Gaton's imminent death, and we are all filled with grief and sorrow because we will miss him greatly. I had shared with him numerous times about my own experiences with death in an effort to decrease any fears he may have experienced. He said he wanted his suffering to be over. He had had a wonderful life, felt he had met the love of his life, Dianne, and considered himself blessed by their relationship.

At that time, I sat with both Gaton and Dianne throughout Gaton's last night of life. I watched them closely and felt so honored that they allowed me to be present for his last hours. He locked eyes on his wife and mouthed to her over and over that he loved her. He waited to die until the only time she looked away. I sat and prayed for them throughout this whole situation. Gaton was home, on hospice, which was his choice.

Death has been described as the demise, the end, the passing, the loss of life. Everyone will die, and everyone we know will face death in the future. This book is based on my experiences as both a patient and a registered nurse. I believe that all life has a purpose and that death is not a permanent end to our existence.

I wrote this book to explain to everyone who reads it what my experience has taught me: Death is not the end. Some will believe me, and others will not. I really don't care, but I have been driven to write my story down so that it can be used to help others when their time happens. I have shared my experiences with many people over the years, but I'm ashamed to say that I hesitated every time I went to write them down. How do you share such a unique, spiritual experience? I felt unable to share things as they happened. I was afraid that I would not remember all the details correctly. How do you describe something so personal, so perfect, and so full of unconditional love? Something happened to me that was so unexpected and so far outside of my cognitive ability to understand. How then can this be described in such a manner to do it justice?

Instead of writing a book, I decided to share my experience one-on-one with terminal patients and their families, and I have done this since it happened in 1996. Every time I felt the Holy Spirit nudge me to share it with someone facing death, I described this experience as a way to explain that death is the beginning not the end. It was also important to me to share that there is no pain in death. I have no fear of death.

I have finally realized that even though sharing my personal experience has helped others one-on-one, many others need to hear or read about how beautiful this experience was; how I felt surrounded by God's unconditional love. I needed to become an empty vessel so that God can speak to your hearts and use me in any way possible.

I dedicate this book to Jesus, my Love, my Lord, my Savior, Yahweh, Abba, Father, Wonderful Counselor, El Shaddai, Elohim, Immanuel, Jehovah, Allah, Adonai, Light of the World, Purifier, and Healer. I absolutely desire every minute of each day to be with Him in heaven. I pray that you prepare yourself to meet Him face to face. He is preparing a place for you. It is life as you can never imagine it. It is like going home in celebration with all those who have gone before you.

This book is an attempt to share with you what this experience was like for me. My hope is that it brings a clearer understanding to families when they experience the death of a loved one. More importantly, my hope is that it brings renewed hope to anyone dying, with or without the support of family or friends. You will not die alone. You will feel the presence of extreme love, warmth, and compassion.

This is the message I was sent back to spread. God will not crash through a door and rescue you; you need to ask Him to come into your life. He has given you free will, and He won't force Himself or His gifts on you. He is always waiting for you to open yourself up to His gifts, although He won't force any of the gifts into your life unless you ask for them. However, His timing is not the same as our perception of time.

We are all connected to God. Life doesn't always go as planned. Jesus has asked us to come follow Him. There is no way I could have gotten through what happened without my relationship with Jesus.

As for me, what happened to me was a life-changing experience. I never expected it; it took me by great surprise. I will try to explain how and why it happened. I pray that God speaks to your heart during the reading of this book and brings great hope to those who are grieving the loss of a loved one.

Acknowledgments

I would like to humbly acknowledge my husband, Stephen Stratoti, who has taught me how unconditional love is displayed, with Jesus as the center of our lives. I wish to also express my deepest affection and appreciation for the foreword he wrote.

It is very important to me to acknowledge two Franciscan women who have had a profound effect upon my life and my faith with Jesus. The first is Sister Mary Ann Shambo, OSF (whose initially professed name was Sr. Judith Marie, and who later became affectionately known as Sr. Judy, the name that I will be using for her throughout this book); together with Sr. Judy is Sr. Barbara Beck, OSF. These two Franciscan Religious have been best friends, kindred spirits, and co-partners in the area of spiritual ministry for over fifty years. Their religious congregation is the Sisters of St. Francis of Philadelphia.

I first met Sr. Judy and Sr. Barbara in 1973, when I was at the St. Agnes School of Nursing. My best friend, Linda, and I met them on an elevator, shortly after the Sisters had come to live at St. Agnes Convent. At that time, they were involved in the Charismatic Renewal as their full-time ministry. The Sisters invited Linda and me to come to the Life in the Spirit seminars, which they were giving. We politely declined, with my friend saying, "Thank you, but we are too busy," and the invite was put on the back burner. However, an incident occurred that compelled us to go, and the rest is history.

But what a history! The Spirit of God moved within the depths of my being, and my faith journey truly began. This journey has led me over hills and mountains, valleys and plains, deserts and flowered meadows, and through it all, Sr. Judy and Sr. Barbara have been my guides.

At one point, Sr. Judy helped me while I wrote my first book, about senior health care, and Sister Barbara's editing and insights have contributed to the contents of this current book. Both Sisters have always been there for me and with me.

But more importantly, each Sister, in her own way and through her own unique love relationship with Jesus, has helped me to recognize and develop my own special, loving relationship with Jesus. They taught me how to listen to Him, to wait upon His time, and to open myself more fully to His presence. In so doing, my natural compassion has become immersed within the compassion of Jesus, which in turn impels me to help others in their need.

Truly, I give thanks to God, with a full and joyous heart, for Sr. Judy and Sr. Barbara, for who they are, and for all they are still doing together (Sr. Judy in heaven and Sr. Barbara on earth) for the glory of God and the good of His people.

Foreword

Every so often, a person comes along who has the gift of seeing the hand of God in everything. Whether it is something good or bad that has happened, these people always ask what God is saying to them. Maybe they can see or hear things that others can't. Most likely it is that they are more *open* to always looking and listening, even when what they are seeing and hearing is hard to bear (or perhaps *especially* when it is hard to bear).

My wife is such a person.

In this book, she shares with us just a little about her journey of faith. I sincerely believe it is an important book because it has the potential of leading others to adopt a similar life of looking and listening, of seeing the hand of God in all things and hearing His call. It can also bring hope and comfort to those who fear death. I've seen her story touch the lives of those who struggle with the burdens of life and the fear of death. It is my prayer that it will touch your life, as well.

Stephen Stratoti

Psalm 139 (A Psalm of David)

The All-knowing and Ever-present God

O Lord, You have probed me and You know me; You know when I sit and when I stand; You understand my thoughts from afar. My journeys and my rest You scrutinize, with all my ways You are familiar. Even before a word is on my tongue, behold, O Lord, You know the whole of it. Behind me and before, You hem me in and rest Your hand upon me. Such knowledge is too wonderful for me; too lofty for me to attain.

Where can I go from Your Spirit? From Your presence, where can I flee? If I go up to the heavens, You are there; if I sink to the nether world, You are present there; if I take the wings of the dawn, if I settle at the farthest limits of the sea, even there Your hand shall guide me, and Your right hand hold me fast. If I say, "Surely the darkness shall hide me, and night shall be my light" – for You darkness itself is not dark, and night shines as the day.

Truly You have formed my inmost being; You knit me in my mother's womb. I give You thanks that I am fearfully, wonderfully made; wonderful are Your works. My soul also You knew full well; nor was my frame unknown to You when I was made in secret, when I was fashioned in the depths of the earth. Your eyes have seen my actions; in Your book they are all written; my days were limited before one of them existed. How weighty are Your designs, O God; how vast the sum of them! Were I to recount them, they would outnumber the sands; did I reach the end of them, I should still be with You.

Probe me, O God, and know my heart; try me, and know my thoughts; See if my way is crooked, and lead me in the way of old.

New American Bible
Catholic Bible Press, a division of Thomas Nelson Publishers
Nashville, Tennessee

My History

Dealing with death and dying was something I discovered I had to do at a very early age. I grew up in a type of *Leave It to Beaver* neighborhood in Swarthmore, Pennsylvania. Everything seemed good to me. My parents were happily married. As children we played ball together, and the boys chased the girls. We rode bikes all around our neighborhood, without any bad incidents or accidents. For grade school, I attended Notre Dame de Lourdes Catholic School, and every day I would walk to school early to visit the church before the school bell rang.

Even though I felt very secure as a young child, I grew up in the sixties, and there were certain happenings that made no sense whatsoever to me. In my early days, students would practice hiding underneath their school desks in the event of a nuclear bomb explosion. The news of the day involved the Cuban missile crisis, the Vietnam War, and people I grew to admire getting shot right in front of us on the TV news.

Death made no sense to me.

When I was around thirteen years old, two of my cousins in my Aunt Rita and Uncle Buddy's family died suddenly. My cousin Dennis was only nine years old when he died on May 2, 1966. He had acute leukemia. Once he was diagnosed, it took less than three weeks for him to die and go to be with God. The week before he was hospitalized, we were at his home playing hide-and-seek; I noticed a lot of black and blue marks on his arms and legs and asked him if someone had hit him. He told me he didn't know why he had them and that no one had hit him. He said he was accident prone and thought that was why he had these bruises. I told my mother, and she discussed Dennis's bruises with Aunt Rita. My aunt said that she was going to speak to the principal of his school to make sure no one was bullying Dennis, as she couldn't understand where the bruises came from, either.

Later that night, when we arrived home, my mother got a call from Aunt Rita, who told her that Dennis started bleeding from his nose and mouth after we had left, so she took him over to the nearest hospital. The doctors did some tests and told her that he had acute leukemia and had very little time to live. My mother slid down to the floor and began sobbing out loud. She kept saying that parents "should not have to bury their children; this was so unfair." My father helped her up, and after finding out about Dennis, he began crying too.

For the next three weeks, Mom went up to the hospital every day to be with Aunt Rita. My mother looked so exhausted. I could hear her crying each night when it was bedtime. I was not prepared to be told that Dennis had less than a week to live. My parents cried when they told us that the only thing left to do was to pray.

I remember my reaction to his sudden death. The emotional grief was unbearable. Although I felt that Dennis was with God, the pain I felt was from watching my family fall apart right in front of me – the emotion, the grief witnessed was real and raw. I never remembered seeing my father and mother both crying, ever, except at these tragedies. I felt their anguish at the loss of my young cousin.

One day before Dennis passed away, I was so sick with grief, I stayed home from school. I asked God to take me instead. I pleaded and cried to Him about the pain of our entire family, especially the grief and loss of my aunt and uncle's son. God did not answer my request. I fell asleep every night, praying that God would take me too. In my innocence, I never realized that there would be even greater grief for my parents if God answered this prayer. I didn't fully understand this situation, but God did.

All of us were in extreme emotional grief. Back then, people dealt with this sort of emotional pain themselves, and so we didn't go to a mental health therapist. There was no hospice support. We just found a way to deal with it to the best of our ability.

As a child, I had no one to go to for comfort because my normal comforters (Mom and Dad) also needed to mourn. Everyone was grieving. How does a child deal with such grief when everyone around them is so devastated? I turned to my God at that time. I yelled at Him, pleading with Him, and said how unfair all of this was. I made it a routine: Before going into school every day, I would stop into the church and say hello to Jesus and ask Him to bless my day. This routine helped me. I knew Jesus would help me find some comfort.

About a year later, on March 21, 1967, just as we were all beginning to feel less pain, Dennis's brother Kevin died; he was only three years old. Now two sons had died, leaving only the eldest brother, Eddie, and my aunt and uncle.

Little Kevin died from a congenital problem with his kidneys. After he died, the children in our family were unable to make any sense out of what had happened. I can remember crying daily to my Jesus. After my aunt and uncle lost their son Dennis, I argued with God about taking Kevin. I beseeched Him to make some sense out of this entire situation for me. Perhaps it was due to all of these losses that I became a nurse, wanting to help people and possibly prevent unnecessary deaths.

I was so distraught at this time that I remember walking into church, looking around to make sure no one was there, and yelling at the cross of Jesus. I screamed at Him that I had witnessed enough death for a child. I begged Him to stop everyone from dying. I pleaded with Him to understand how difficult it was for us humans here on earth. I also remember that I cried myself to sleep every night for a long time, but I never stopped believing He'd be merciful.

Because of all the personal trauma and death surrounding our family, I found myself wondering at an early age what my purpose in life was. Whenever I prayed like this, from my heart, expressing my feelings to God, I would end up quiet and listening. I felt an ever so light cool mist envelope me. I felt this was God's spirit telling me that everything was going to be all right. I also received a sweet scent of roses during my prayer at this time; when this happened, I immediately felt that I could imagine physically resting in the arms of Jesus.

Most families face death at some point, but in our family, there were three main events that forced me to deal with death and dying at a very early age.

The 1960s were so upside-down.

I believe that our nation as a whole was negatively impacted by the evil that surrounded our country. On November 22, 1963, when I was ten, all of America witnessed, over and over again, President John F. Kennedy being shot right in front of us on TV; the brutality of death was more real to everyone during that terribly tragic time. We had never seen anything so horrible, so raw, and so evil on television. Our school had assigned everyone to watch the president's speech in Texas that day. President Kennedy was the first Catholic president of the United States. None of us really wanted to watch this, but we had been directed by our teacher to write a paper on the content of the speech to be presented that next week. Instead, we witnessed pure evil.

Rather than present papers, our school did their best at crises counseling because of what everyone witnessed. Even if you didn't stop and watch the motorcade, it was on every news station in America; we were forced to relive this agonizing moment, time and time again. This whole tragic situation happened a day before my tenth birthday. I remember crying for days. Our class was asked to pray for the president's family members. We watched as the Kennedy family, including their little children, buried their father, our president. What a sacrifice to witness. It made no sense.

All of the Sisters and teachers were crying, our parents were crying, and so as children, we felt the extreme grief of all those around us; our nation was in mourning. When I got home from school that day, I wanted to play baseball but couldn't because it somehow would seem disrespectful to President Kennedy's memory. I was only ten years old when he died. I spent my birthday that year watching his funeral over and over again.

In 1963, there was a march to the Lincoln Memorial in Washington DC. Reverend Martin Luther King Jr. gave the "I Have a Dream" speech. He was an activist for human rights and social justice. He won the Nobel Peace Prize in 1964 at the age of thirty-five. And then four years later, someone shot him. On April 4, 1968, I watched the assassination of the Reverend King, who had gone to Memphis, Tennessee, in support of striking garbage workers there. I asked my father, "Why do people hate so much?" He had no answer and didn't understand this, either, and so I continued to pray.

I vividly remember seeing the assassination of Robert Kennedy on June 5, 1968, over and over, channel after channel. There was no getting away from the story. People all over the country were crying. I felt so bad for the Kennedy family.

I remember seeing the funeral of RFK at St. Patrick's Cathedral. I wondered to myself how this family could cope with such a loss and how the world could be so violent.

I often talked with my father about the Vietnam War. I opposed war in every form. I felt afraid of the war in Vietnam, which we heard about time and time again on TV. I was also afraid of the antiwar demonstrations we saw on TV. I wondered where it was all leading us. Young boys I knew in the neighborhood were drafted to Vietnam and then came back in body bags. My own father spoke out against this war and informed my brothers that if it ever came to them being called to the draft, he had friends in Canada, and he would send them there to remain safe. He never believed in violence or war. He was a peacemaker his whole life.

I prayed the Rosary every night and usually fell asleep with my beads in my hand. I would wake up every day, asking Jesus to help me get through life. It was hard for my whole family to cope with these sudden deaths. No one knows how to prepare for death, especially the death of a child. I remember telling Jesus that something more had to be done to help people understand and deal with death.

None of the adults I knew could cope with either sudden death or prolonged suffering. No one knew what to say to us kids. We were like sponges, absorbing their emotional pain and suffering. I wanted, I longed, to be with Jesus and away from this life.

Death was very scary to me. After both of my cousins died, their grandfather on Aunt Rita's side of the family committed suicide. I heard that he shot himself in the head because of the grief at the loss of his two grandchildren. He had lived across the street from Aunt Rita, and being the oldest Italian daughter, she took care of him daily and made sure he felt connected. She found him dead, lying on his couch, so once again, our family was in mourning. I remember people speaking about how God did not sanction suicide.

I wondered as a child if this loving, caring grandfather who missed his grandchildren so much would go to heaven or hell for his suicide. I could never believe that my God would condemn someone who was so depressed by life's twists and turns or would send them to hell. My God would look at the whole situation and bring him into His love. He would speak to his heart and empathize with his emotional and spiritual pain.

As children, we tried to support our cousin, Eddie. After all, he had just lost both brothers and now his grandfather. We were trying to keep him occupied and keep things light. We didn't know how to act, so we tried to play with him and make him laugh. He spent a lot of time with our family after the death of his brothers. Our home was like a retreat for him. We hoped growing up with the closeness of our family would be healing for him.

Again, the pain I saw in my aunt seemed unbearable. She said she felt like a zombie getting through life, one minute at a time. No one was untouched by these tragic situations. Her husband, Uncle Buddy, had developed a very bad heart condition and had to have a pacemaker. He died several years later at a young age.

So now, Aunt Rita was left alone, raising Eddie without a father. How she carried on, we will never know. However, she never stopped believing in Jesus throughout her life; even with all her tragedies, she focused on Jesus's love. She has a strong faith and a good relationship with Jesus. Because of this, she looks forward to seeing her family again after she dies.

Aunt Rita had asked someone to take pictures of her son in his coffin. This was unheard of at that time. Dennis was buried in his Holy Communion suit, and Kevin was buried in his baptismal gown. They looked so innocent, so peaceful – just like they were sleeping, without a care in the world.

How does a child make any sense out of something like this? Most children never experience death surrounding them like we did. We were told that death is a part of life. We were told that we all needed to be there for Aunt Rita and Uncle Buddy. I never wanted to deal with death again.

Why Nursing School?

I went to Cardinal O'Hara High School. For three years, I was into business as a point of interest. The year I was a senior, I was elected the president of the Future Business Leaders of America. As a senior, I decided to become a nurse. I thought that all of my past experiences would help me work through my emotions regarding death and dying. One day, my business teacher cornered me and asked why I chose nursing to study; she said I had what it takes to be a leader in the business world and expected great things from me.

I told her about my cousins and all that my family had experienced, saying, "I need to better understand why these things happened like they did."

She said, "I don't want you to give up on having your own business someday."

I hugged her and promised that I would not give up that dream.

I don't know if she ever understood what I was trying to convey at that time. I didn't understand my being drawn to nursing, either, but I was. Once I got into nursing school, which was St. Agnes in South Philadelphia, I began visiting the chapel daily. I prayed for direction, to be open, to be taught whatever it was I was supposed to learn. I also remember the fear of death creeping into my dreams and the deeply felt grief I had stored during my childhood.

I asked myself how I would cope with a patient who was dying. I didn't think I could do this. I called my mother every week and spoke with my dad whenever things resurfaced, asking them to understand that nursing may not be for me. They would listen to me for hours and then gently remind me that there is a reason for everything; if I wanted to quit the nursing school, they would come up and get me. Once I heard that they understood and would come for me if things got too tough, I began to relax. Whenever things in nursing school got too serious, I was the one student to crack a joke or bring some humor into the situation, just to ease what we were experiencing. Looking back, I guess it was a way for me to cope.

I was the first student nurse in my class to have a patient die while caring for her. She was Italian, about eighty-nine years old with white and gray hair, and as cute as could be. One day, after I helped her with her care, she decided she would take a short nap.

That morning, she had written a letter to her family and gave it to me to give to them.

I patted the letter she had given me and said, "You should be the one to give it to them."

She smiled and said, "I will be gone by the time they arrive."

I frowned and asked, "What do you mean?"

"I had a dream," she said, leaning forward, her eyes bright. "I am going to die today."

"Are you in any pain?" I asked, searching her face and checking her vitals for any indication of pain.

"No." She smiled again, watching me. Then she said, "Jesus visited me."

I then asked her about her dream, and she said that Jesus visited her and told her that she would be crowned in glory that day. She saw herself dressed in a beautiful, brilliant white robe. I was only eighteen at the time; I smiled and proceeded to do everything I was assigned to do. I thought to myself, *Okay, please don't die on me today.*

After I helped her dress, I got her into her Geri chair and asked if I could wheel her toward the nurses' desk. She said yes. Once I got her there, she looked fine, so I proceeded to document what was done that day for her. When I looked up from her chart, she looked peaceful but didn't appear to be breathing. I rushed over to her, gently took her out of the chair and put her down on the floor, and began CPR. I knew that

I was not going to get her back. She had prepared herself to die, and she did. Back then, no one had advance directives; every patient was considered a full code. But I knew deep down inside that no amount of CPR would work, as it was her time.

When her family came in to see her, I gave the letter to them, and when they read it, they cried. They shared the letter with me, which restated that she knew she was going to leave them that day. She wrote that she had seen Jesus and was told she would be with Him soon. Her description of her dream was beautiful. Angels were present. Her letter spoke of her being presented to Jesus in a beautiful, brilliant white gown and a crown being placed on her head. At that time, I didn't know what to think about death. I didn't think it was fair to me to have her die while in my care. I went into the chapel at the hospital and spoke with God about that whole experience. I always told Him how I felt when something unexpected happened.

Shortly thereafter, I began to realize that many of the other student nurses had little experience dealing with death and the dying. Because of all my family experiences, I could deal with the tragedies we saw while in school with humor and lots of prayer.

I remember happier times prior to my cousins dying. It was traumatic to witness all the adults in our lives crying and holding onto one another. Things seemed so out of control. It was hard for us children who were grieving; we couldn't envision death but slowly began to realize that our lives would change forever. The world continues to move forward after people we know die. Sometimes, we get stuck emotionally when we are not able to resolve our grief.

After my cousins died, we tried to act like nothing had changed. I remember being told how to act. Not wanting to cause any further grief for our parents, we held our anger in instead of expressing it verbally. This was not helpful to us at all. Because our parents had trouble coping with their loss, no one was being attentive to our responses. I know now that this was not purposeful. They had their hands full dealing with other adults in extreme grief.

I believe that a mother who has lost a child will never stop grieving. I would never underestimate the power of a parent's love. If parents have their own emotions in order, they are better able to help a child through this type of loss. No one can take away the pain of a loss, but our pain doesn't have to keep us from reaching out to a child. As children, we saw everyone crying; they were very emotional. If we saw our parents with tears in their eyes, they would dismiss them by saying that dust had blown into their eyes. Our parents and family members were almost numb to their pain, dismissing their grief while trying to stay busy arranging the funeral. Sharing emotional connections and listening to a child's feelings, validating those feelings and understanding that all behaviors have meaning, are all ways we can help a child who is grieving.

I believe that children should be told as soon as possible when someone in the family dies, to prevent them from hearing it from another source. An honest explanation of what happened is needed in language that is easily understood by the child. A child who has had someone die needs to interpret the death literally. My cousin was told that his brother was "asleep with the angels." For the longest time, he prayed that he would wake up and come back home.

Parents need to understand that children may have questions for weeks or months; they will seek out reassurance that the story hasn't changed. Children will cry, will feel sad and depressed, and may want to cry with their parents.

Without even realizing it, my cousin and brothers and I looked for ways to help express our emotions. We drew pictures, we played hide-and-seek, and we all wanted to talk with each other about what we were hearing our parents whisper throughout the home.

Michael's Story

One of my most vivid memories from St. Agnes School of Nursing was while I was in my pediatric rotation at the naval base in South Philadelphia. This involved a Sr. Immaculata, OSF (known as Sr. Mac). She was our *Fundamentals In Nursing* teacher and had assigned me to take care of a small boy named Michael, for my pediatric rotation. She explained that Michael was in isolation and that I would be assigned to his care during my three months of pediatrics. My experience with Michael changed my life forever.

I said, "Sister, what's wrong with him?"

Sr. Mac promptly informed me that he had leukemia.

Upon hearing this, I felt my knees shaking and my body went limp. I thought I was going to pass out. When she saw how pale I had become, she rushed over to me and had one of the students get me some orange juice. I think she thought that I was having a low blood sugar situation, but in reality, I was reliving my cousin's death from acute leukemia.

I replied quickly, "Sister, I can't take care of this little boy because I've never been able to deal with my own cousin's death from leukemia at the very same age."

I thought she would be very understanding of the situation.

Instead, she promptly stated, "Cassidy [that was my maiden name, and she called everyone by their last name], if you don't take care of this young boy with leukemia, then you may as well go back to the school, pack up your things, and call for a ride home. You will never make it as a nurse."

"Sister," I asked, "please, can you reassign me to another patient?" But she refused.

She told me that I should at least put on a gown, gloves, and mask to meet young Michael before I made my decision to leave nursing.

I did what she asked and carefully gowned, gloved, and masked prior to going into the isolation room. Lying in front of me was a bald-headed nine-year-old boy, who greeted me with a broad smile.

He asked, "Who are you? I'm glad they sent you; I'm so bored."

I was able to see past his leukemia to realize that this little boy was just that: a boy who had been dealt a bad situation. He proceeded to tell me about himself.

Michael informed me that he had leukemia for the past seven years. During those seven years, he had been in and out of the hospital, sometimes several times a year. He stated, "I love baseball; it's my favorite sport." He said he had hoped to get out of the hospital after chemotherapy to play one more game that season. He also stated that he wanted to be treated normal, like other kids.

I promptly sat down beside him and tuned into what he was saying. I heard his need to be listened to. He talked to me and shared with me about his family, why he was there, how he knew all of the staff, and he really didn't like it when the doctor came in because he was always "so serious."

Michael said that he wanted to make the doctor and staff members laugh. He liked to play practical jokes. He admitted to me that this time, he was really worried about his mom and dad, as they seemed so sad when they came to visit. He said that when he told his famous jokes that they used to laugh at, they didn't laugh anymore. He asked me if I knew any new jokes, and so we shared some. He said, "I will let you know if I get any laughs using them."

Michael's isolation room had a large window that allowed him to see people passing in the hallways. He wanted attention from them; he wanted them to laugh and wave as they passed by. He didn't know how to reach them. I decided to have some fun with him that day, so I took a pad of lined paper and asked him to help me roll each paper into a ball. It took a while to do this. He laughed because we had paper balls all over his bed. I then took the trash can in his room, and we played baseball, using our arms as bats; after that, we decided to play basketball. Of course, I let him win. It was good to see him smile.

When it was time to go, I told him I would be back the next day. I left his room; removed my isolation gown, gloves, and mask; and waved through the glass to him so he could see what I looked like under all that equipment. He smiled and waved back. I then went to our exit conference, where students had to tell Sr. Mac what diagnoses their assigned patient had and how they would approach a plan of care.

Sister asked me how everything went.

I told her, "So far so good."

She knew about the play time, as she had passed by in the hallway to look in several times. I hadn't even noticed. She asked me how I came up with a game so quickly, and I told her I thought about my cousin during the entire time I was in the room and prayed for him to intercede for this boy. She could tell I wanted to come back the next day, and I asked her if I could bring in a game for Michael to play. She told me I had to wipe it down with alcohol and leave it inside the room. Later on, I went to the hospital chapel and prayed for this young boy's total healing. I pleaded with God to let him live and have the ultimate healing. I spent hours praying; I cried and felt peaceful afterwards.

That night, I slept like a baby. I felt that God had heard me, and I had overcome my fear of death relating to my cousin. I really felt like I had grown emotionally once I entered Michael's room. On a weekly basis, Sr. Mac advised me on not getting too close and to be realistic with my approaches. She knew about how helpless I had felt when my cousin died suddenly. She also knew that I was getting very close to Michael, very quickly.

The next day, I bought a plastic gun that shot darts with rubber tips on the end. I carefully washed it with alcohol, and after waving to Michael, gowning, gloving, and putting my mask on, I entered his room and held the gun behind me to surprise him.

He said again, "I'm so bored."

I then pulled out the gun and pretended to shoot him. He began giggling and became so excited that he rolled around on his bed, smiling.

He then asked, "Can I shoot anyone who passed by the window?"

I said yes, and he proceeded to shoot his rubber-tipped projectiles at his glass window as other staff walked by so seriously. He tired of this after about ten minutes because he couldn't get anyone's attention.

He then spotted the doctor gowning and gloving to enter his room. He smiled and asked, "Can I shoot my gun at the doctor's head?"

I warned him to not hit him in the eye and then said, "Why not?"

He squealed and took aim. The minute the doctor entered his room, he shot the rubber-tipped dart and hit him right in the forehead. Michael laughed so hard, I thought he was going to fall out of his bed. The doctor took the dart that was stuck on his forehead, rolled his eyes, and smiled.

He then asked, "Who gave you this?"

Michael replied, "Why do you need to know?"

The doctor responded that he just wanted to know what other surprises were in store for him when he visits, and then he laughed and returned the dart to the boy.

The physician told Michael, "It is so good to see you laughing and playful. But I am afraid I have some bad news to discuss with you."

He turned to me and asked who I was.

I explained that I was a second-year student nurse at St. Agnes School of Nursing and told him that if he wanted me to leave the room so he could speak to Michael, I would be happy to do so.

Michael said, "No, I want you here. Please hold my hand."

I thought it was odd that the physician would speak to Michael before talking to his parents, but this doctor had taken care of him for the last seven years and knew the family well.

And so, I held his hand while his doctor explained that this may be the year that he doesn't get out of the hospital to play baseball.

I remember crying behind the mask I wore. Michael looked so sad. He asked the doctor if he had talked with his mom and dad yet.

The doctor said no.

He told the doctor that his parents would be in soon and that "you better be the one to tell them I won't be able to play on the Little League team this year." After the doctor left the room, little Michael told me, "I'm really tired and want to be alone."

I went to lunch as he was falling asleep.

It was very emotional to watch this nine-year-old boy struggling with his leukemia. Toward the end of my pediatric rotation, he said, "I don't want to be sick, and I don't want any more chemotherapy because it makes me sick." I sat and listened to him that afternoon, holding his hand, thinking how brave this little boy was throughout this whole ordeal.

When I went back to the dorms that night, I was so upset. I felt I needed to do something. I called one of the novice Sisters up, who was also a student nurse; she was going to a prayer meeting that night.

I asked her to pray for little Michael to be totally healed. She told me that there were going to be thousands of people praying, because a healer by the name of Brother Panky was speaking about healing of the body, mind, and spirit. She asked me to come and sit in as proxy for prayers for little Michael. She informed me that there would be praying in tongues. I told her that I didn't believe in people praying in tongues. I told her that it frightened me. She asked me to come and said it was for Michael; I should think about what was best for him. I kept picturing this little angel in my head and thinking about how very sick he was and finally decided that I would go with her. I felt I had nothing to lose by asking for this miracle of total healing.

That night, at seven o'clock, I entered the church and stood with my back against the wall, as it was standing room only. I believe that if anyone saw me, they would say that I looked like a deer caught in headlights. There were thousands of people in this church, which was not far from the naval base hospital where Michael was in isolation. People were singing, chanting, clapping their hands, jumping, and dancing.

I told the Franciscan Sister who brought me, "This can't be for real."

She told me that it was. Sister told me that praying in tongues was a gift from the Holy Spirit and a purer way to pray. I had never heard of it happening in a Catholic church before. I had read about it in the Bible regarding Pentecost, when the Holy Spirit came down upon Jesus's followers, and they prayed in all different languages, but never in my life had I met anyone with this gift. I was scared.

That night, after Brother Panky spoke about healing the body, mind, and spirit, he invited people up to the altar so that he could pray over them. He said that prayer teams were ready to pray for healing. Sister kept urging me to go up for prayer, but I was hugging the wall so hard because I did not want to go. I thought, *She must be nuts.* But I waited, and waited, and waited as others were prayed over. People were falling down onto the ground. Sister explained that this was called being "slain in the Spirit." No one got hurt, as other team members would help catch them and lower them gently to the floor.

Finally, I saw Brother Panky pray for the entire group, and with one downward swoop of his arm and hand, whole groups were falling left and right. He looked at me and said someone had come to pray for a small boy with a serious illness. Sister looked at me and said, "Go on." I said, "No, I'm not the one he's speaking about."

Just then, someone else got up and went to be prayed for.

The end was near, and the large crowd began to disperse. Sister walked me up to introduce me to Brother Panky. He was a powerfully gifted person, and he looked right into my eyes and my soul.

He said, "Why did you come here tonight?"

I said, "To pray for a small boy who has leukemia. I wanted to ask God to heal him totally."

Brother Panky said, "Do you want to sit in proxy for him?"

I told him that I didn't really understand what that meant, and he explained that it would be like Michael was there himself, receiving graces and answers to prayers.

I answered yes.

Brother Panky immediately asked those around me to help him with praying in the Spirit. I began standing in the middle of about eight people, and as they prayed over me, my heart cried. Tears were falling because of this young boy and his suffering. I began to open up my heart to Jesus. I begged God to heal him completely, body, mind, and spirit. I went from my standing position to a kneeling position and felt a surge go through my body that is hard to describe. I felt like I was anointed with holy oil and could feel it slowly cover me, from my head to my toes My whole being was warm, and I felt enveloped in love.

I felt peace, joy, and filled with love; I was no longer a skeptic regarding this praying in tongues. All of a sudden, I began to sing in tongues so loud, and it was so freeing. I kept saying to myself, *This is nuts, this can't be happening to me.* It felt like a long time had passed; I can't remember crying so much in front of people I didn't know. I felt woozy when I tried to get back up on my feet. Brother Panky directed someone to get me a chair.

He explained to me that the gift of tongues can open up prayer to a person like never before. While you might pray a few minutes at a time here and there, when you pray in tongues, it is easy to go for hours praying and worshiping. This gift creates a direct connection between your spirit and the Holy Spirit, who prays within you and empowers your prayer to be prayed in a language you never studied or learned.

Brother Panky told me that my prayers were going to be answered, that little Michael would soon be totally healed and be with the Lord in Paradise. When I heard this, I told him, "This is not what I was praying for; I wanted him healed here on earth. He can't die. That's not what I asked for."

Brother Panky told me that after we are totally healed on earth, we are with the Lord fully, on another spiritual plain. He told me that death is another path into a fuller life in the Spirit.

I was so confused. I thought, *Maybe I am hearing this wrong. I don't know these people; maybe they are wrong.*

I opened up my eyes, looked around the church, and realized that after Brother Panky started praying over me, hundreds of people came back into the church and were circled around me, laying hands on each other and on those praying over me. It was extremely powerful. But I still left that night wanting Michael to be healed completely. I wanted him healed physically.

That week, I met two new Franciscan Sisters who were just moving into the convent. They both looked friendly enough, but I quietly joked with my roommate that "more penguins were coming" (they both had black and white habits on). They overheard my comment, and the taller one, Sr. Judy Shambo (OSF), asked me what I said. I told her my comment was made only in jest and meant no harm.

She looked at me and said, "You and I are going to get to know each other very well." This turned out to be very true.

I introduced myself and told her that it was nice to meet her.

Then she began to tell me that she and the other Sister, Sr. Barbara Beck (OSF), both Franciscans, were involved in a ministry within the charismatic renewal and were going to give Life in the Spirit seminars. She asked me and my roommate to come on Wednesdays, since there was only a small group coming at that time. I told her that we were really busy with school and assignments and that I didn't think we would be coming.

When she left the elevator, she smiled and said, "See you both on Wednesday night."

I whispered, "No, you won't," and waved back.

The very next week, I went back to see Michael, as assigned. He looked very pale, and his lips were getting purple. After I gowned and gloved and applied my mask, I went in to sit with him. He opened up his eyes and told me that he was so happy to see me again. I told him about the prayers the other night; I explained that I sat in proxy for him and that I was assured that he was going to be totally healed: body, mind, and spirit.

He very quietly asked me to understand that he "needed to do what Jesus told him to do," but that he was afraid that his "Mommy and Daddy were going to be too sad."

I asked him to help me understand what he meant and that maybe if I understood, I could help him.

He whispered, "Last night, I had a dream. Jesus was in my room. He was dressed like Superman and had a great big cape on. He took me with Him, and we flew all through the clouds. He told me to just reach out and touch him and that I would never fall. I flew right next to Him and didn't fall because I touched His hand. We talked about everything: my family, Mom and Dad, my brothers and sisters, and how much I was going to miss playing baseball. I told him I was hungry, and he asked me what I wanted. I missed the hot dogs and candy from the ballpark, so I asked Him if I could have that. He scooped up a cloud in His hand, and there was a hot dog, just like I loved it. Then he scooped another part of a cloud and gave me cotton candy. Then He told me He had a surprise for me. We flew to an area that looked like clouds, but when He moved His hands, it was a professional baseball field. Michael said that he was so excited because all of the players were in place, waiting to play baseball with him and Jesus."

Michael said that Jesus introduced him to some of the players. Real baseball players and some angels played against Jesus and Michael. Every ball pitched to Michael was a hit, and he got so many home runs. He didn't want this to end.

He said, "We played for a long time, and then before I knew it, Jesus and I were back here in my room." He told me that he needed to share this with me and wanted me to help his mommy and daddy to understand "that it is my time to go back to heaven with Jesus and that everyone will be seeing each other again soon."

As this child told his dream to me, I was crying underneath my face mask. I thought, *No, this is not what I prayed for. Please God, let him live.* I remember thinking, *Who am I to tell his parents that it is his time to go back to heaven with Jesus? I can't do this; I am only eighteen years old. I don't know what to say. I can't do this.*

Michael then asked me to tell his dream in detail to his parents when they came. He stated that they knew how close we had become and that they would accept this coming from me. He told me that he was going to send me letters through airmail after he died. He begged me to help his parents accept what was going to happen and understand that he would be seeing them again soon. He felt that he was sticking around because they couldn't let go. He felt that he needed their permission to die.

I made up an excuse to leave the room, stripped my isolation gown off, and went straight to Sr. Mac. I told her everything. I remember being so emotionally upset and pacing back and forth while speaking with her. I explained to her that my prayers were for "total healing of body, mind, and spirit. Not for him to die." I asked her what I should do.

She said, "Cassidy, for whatever reason, God wants you to help this young boy, and you just have to do it."

I said, "But Sister, I can't. Who am I to tell this family that their son isn't going home this time?" I remember saying, "This assignment isn't fair, I told you about losing my cousin at the same age to leukemia." I was in a panic and didn't feel able to follow through on telling his parents. I felt so inadequate.

Just then, Michael's mom and dad came into the solarium and began taking off their coats.

Sr. Mac said, "Speak up, Cassidy."

I formally introduced myself, and once I did, Michael's mother grabbed me and hugged me and thanked me for all that I had been doing with her son. She said that Michael told them that we played games together; whenever I was taking care of him, he felt blessed. She told me that he told her she needed to speak with me about something very important. I paced back and forth. I really didn't know how to begin. I kept having difficulty believing that God would use me to deliver this kind of bad news.

I began to sweat, listening to my own fears. I stammered in the beginning, trying to tell them that Michael had a dream and that he wanted me to share his dream with them both. They told me that in the past, when Michael had dreams, he always had trouble remembering them. They told me they knew he would recover again, as baseball season was right around the corner.

Their statements revealed what they wanted to happen, rather than what was happening; I realized why Michael wanted me to be the one to tell them that Jesus had visited him and what that visit was all about.

I asked them to please have a seat. I explained that even though Michael and I had been working together for only three months, that we had grown close. Then I began to describe Michael's dream. As I shared his dream, I began to cry. I told both parents that Michael did not want to disappoint them this time, but he wanted to go home with

Jesus and play ball in heaven with His angels. "He is afraid to tell you this himself," I explained, "because you always tell him not to worry and he can beat this."

His father was speechless. His mother had tears running down her cheeks. She said, "Jesus flew with him through the clouds? He played ball with him? Oh my God, we have been keeping him here because we don't want him to go. Every year, we pushed him to either get chemo or radiation and a bone marrow transplant because we wanted to keep him with our family.

"We have eight children total," she continued, "but for the last seven years of our lives, everything focused around Michael."

"He wants permission from you both to go," I said. "Please speak with him and tell him that you know about his dream. He is very weak and can barely speak; he wants to say goodbye until he sees you all again in heaven. He said that this is what Jesus told him, that you will all be together again in heaven."

Both parents hugged each other. His father called home and arranged to have a family member bring up the rest of the family, while Michael's mother went into his room with gowns, gloves, and mask. He looked like death. His color was pale, and lips were purple even with oxygen. I went in to say goodbye and slowly bent down to kiss him.

He whispered, "Did you tell them?"

"Yes," I said. "They know, Michael. Don't worry; your mother was very excited that Jesus and the angels played baseball with you, and that you want to go to be with Jesus."

Michael's mother sat next to his bed and leaned in to tell him that it was all right to go. She said, "You know, Michael, we have had you here on earth for over nine years. You have been such a good son. Jesus is the One Who sent you to us. Of course, we want you to be with Him in heaven."

Michael's brothers and sisters all arrived. A family meeting was held in the solarium down the hall. Michael's mother came out to get each child to say goodbye to him one by one and to speak privately with him one last time. Once this was done, everyone came back into the room; we all joined hands, and the family prayed the Lord's Prayer together. Michael was barely breathing.

My ride waited extra-long for me that night, because I had to be back at the dormitory by a certain time. I asked Michael's mother to call me when they left and to let me know how he was doing. She said she would.

I couldn't eat that night; I couldn't sleep, either. I had many thoughts going through my brain. I argued with God, Jesus in particular. I asked Him why things like this happen to little children like Michael. The pain in my heart was unbearable. I felt like my cousin Dennis was dying all over again. *I can't do this*, I kept telling myself. *This profession isn't for me. I don't want to tell parents that their child is going to die.* And I blamed myself for his impending death because I went and prayed for a total healing. Who did I think I was? Why would God put me smack dab in the middle of this tragedy? It was beyond my comprehension.

I called those two new Sisters in the convent and asked them to pray for this child and family. They asked me if I wanted to talk more about the situation, and I said no. I was afraid that if I spoke to anyone about what was happening, I would become unglued.

Later that night, Michael's mother called and thanked me for telling her about the dream.

She said, "We all surrounded Michael's bed right after you left. We decided that it was all right to take off all of the isolation equipment, gowns, and masks. We wanted him to see us again. Everyone told him that it was okay to go and be with Jesus. We told him that we were going to really miss him but that we knew that we would see each other again in heaven. He slipped into a deep sleep, and we stayed with him until he had no pulse or respirations. We all felt God's presence at his bedside. We know that he is happy and in a place full of love. We all know we will see him again."

I began to cry. I was lucky no one was near me. I thanked her for her call and hung up. I slowly made it back to my room and sobbed into my pillow. I cried myself to sleep, praying for the family and feeling overwhelmed with sadness. Around eleven o'clock, I opened my eyes and saw a sudden flash of light in my room. I was scared to death. I felt a presence like I had never experienced before. Some "being" was in my room.

He was brilliant in color (the brightest white); he also looked scared himself but angelic, brilliant, and full of light. I felt that he didn't come to hurt me but to deliver his message. I was so scared, I shut my eyes tight and worked my way over to the wall to flip on the light switch to see what really was happening. I felt a cool breeze pass by me. When I flipped on the lights, nothing was there. I ran down the hallway to the phone and called the convent. I told the Sister who answered the phone that I needed to talk to Sr. Judy, the nun I met in the elevator; I said it was an emergency. Sr. Judy came to the phone, and I rapidly told her what had been happening to me.

Sr. Judy tried to calm me down; she said, "Whenever something like this happens, all you have to do is ask in the name of Jesus if this situation is from the Lord."

I said, "Sister, I need to study these things. Too much is happening to me, and I don't understand what's going on."

She told me it could have been an angel visiting or even Michael and to not be afraid. She invited me to their seminar to learn more about what I had experienced that week, and I decided to go. In hindsight, I do believe it was little Michael coming to me to tell me that he was all right. After all, he did say he would send me a message.

Sr. Judith and Sr. Barbara both took me under their wings and became my spiritual directors after this experience. They taught me many things about prayer, how to live in the present moment, and how to accept whatever was happening as a life lesson. They opened my eyes up to the importance of being in communion with God the Father, Son, and Holy Spirit. They helped me accept things as they unfolded before me and understand that God was truly real and wants only what was best for me. Because of their guidance and prayers, I did go through the Life in the Spirit seminars, and I began praying for anyone who asked for prayers. I also became involved in a healing ministry through their prayers and guidance.

Michael's death helped me to better understand what I had experienced as a child when my cousins died suddenly. My search for meaning in this life experience helped me open up to the gifts of the Holy Spirit; it began a sincere walk with God. God has a special love for all humankind. He helps us through all of the tragedies in our life experiences and will never leave us. He accepts you right where you are in life. He knows how you feel, but if you are open to it, He has a life lesson to teach through each experience. God continues to love us unconditionally, even with all our flaws. He waits for us to be ready to listen. It has been my life experience that when I am ready to listen, He speaks to my heart and soul.

I now realize that everything I have experienced in my life has been for a purpose. I needed to feel the pain and deep loss of my cousins. I needed to experience how my parents and Aunt Rita's family felt to understand such deep emotional grief.

Sudden Death

After graduation from nursing school, I worked for several years in a burn unit. As an RN, I would pick up burn victims in a helicopter and transport them to our special unit for immediate evaluation and care. This was beyond critical care nursing; the unit allowed me to grow in my nursing background beyond measure. The time I spent as a burn nurse was so important in understanding how the body is affected, how lives change so drastically when you are seriously burned. And of course, I saw many people die in the burn unit, even though we did everything we could to try to save our patients.

The physicians, nurses, and techs trained and worked side by side to help heal our burn patients. We knew within seventy-two hours if a burn patient would make it or not. Sepsis would creep in and create a total body/organ shutdown much of the time. One day, a thirty-year-old fireman was brought in. He was trapped in a fire and was burned over 95 percent of his body. He was unrecognizable. He could still speak and asked me to come close to him so I could hear what he said. He couldn't see, so he began by asking me if anyone else from his family was present. I told him it was just me. He then begged me to put a pillow over his nose and to kill him. He didn't want his wife to see him like this. He never wanted his kids to see him like this.

"Please," he cried, "please listen to me. You know I am going to die anyway; just end it sooner. Give me some dignity; don't let my wife see me like this."

I gave him more pain medication and asked him if he believed in

God. He said yes. I asked him if I could pray with him, and he said, "Yes, please."

He begged God to take him as soon as possible. After we prayed, his wife came in. She was around twenty-eight years old. She introduced herself to me and began to cry when she asked to see him. She didn't realize that he was right in front of her, as his body was wrapped in gauze; his body had swollen to triple its size.

He was unrecognizable. She spoke to him and asked if he could hear her. She told him how much she loved him and that it didn't matter that he was burned, she would still love him. She begged him to get better and to try as hard as possible because they had a son and another baby on the way, and they all needed him. He didn't answer her at all. I explained that he was just medicated for pain and that she should come back in an hour or so to speak with him again. She was very uncomfortable in the unit, and I could tell that seeing all the burn victims was making her very upset. She decided to leave and said that she would be back in the morning to see him. I got her to agree to come in to see a counselor so that she had someone to speak with about her feelings regarding this tragedy.

Once she left, I went to check his vital signs; he whispered, "Is she gone?" I told him yes. He then told me that he couldn't speak with her about his situation because he wanted her to think that he never woke up.

He implied that she could handle his death much better if she thought he had no pain and went comfortably when he died.

I couldn't believe my ears, listening to this fireman. In the midst of all his agony and pain, knowing the statistics about sepsis and what burns do to a body, he was thinking about his wife's reaction and wanted to comfort her by acting like he was knocked out and unable to respond. He told me about their relationship; he shared how strong she was and that she didn't think she could raise their children by herself, but she would be fine. He told me that he had taken out a life insurance policy that would help her with paying bills and his burial. I asked him what made him think he was going to die.

He said, "You know I'm dying; you know that no one's body can be burned like mine and not die. It's just a matter of time."

He was right. We used to work twelve-hour shifts. When I went home that night, I stopped to say goodbye to him before leaving. He thanked me for not telling his wife that he could speak because he really didn't want her to know the pain he was in.

When I returned that next day, he had already passed. Back in those days, we were sent out to pick up the burn victims; we started IVs on fire victims when we could and quickly got them back to the burn unit to tub them, wrap their wounds, and medicate them for the most severe pain.

Our team began each shift with prayer. We prayed out loud while treating each burn victim and wrapping their wounds and ended each day with prayers, hoping that we would see our patients that next day. Many times, we prayed over our patients as a team. We never forced this; we were asked. Sometimes, a patient would hear us praying over another patient and then would ask the team to pray for them too. Even patients who came in as agnostic asked us to pray for them, just to cover all bases.

Working in this burn unit was the most educational experience of my nursing career. The team of physicians, RNs, medics, and aides were all trained together from the start, and we all worked like a well-oiled machine. Time is of the essence when dealing with a burn victim. Each week, we met with a psychologist to understand how our work was affecting our emotions; after a while, we all began to feel the losses we experienced. We also understood why a burn patient would not want to have their loved ones see them in such pain. We recognized the anguish and complete despair we saw on the faces of the families as we carried them through these terrible times.

Stay with Me

After attending St. Agnes School of Nursing for three years, I received my RN license. I worked as an RN for several years and then decided to go back to college to get my bachelor's degree in nursing. During this time, I joined several prayer groups and participated in healing ministry. God continued to use the healing gifts He gave me, and with each new situation, my walk with God grew deeper.

When I was twenty-six, I took a trip to Paris, Rome, and Israel. It was more like a spiritual pilgrimage. On this spiritual journey, I was privileged to visit San Giovanni Rotondo, which included the church where St. Padre Pio had his congregation. St. Padre Pio was a priest who had been given the five wounds of Jesus, referred to as the stigmata. He was also given the gift of bilocation and could see into the soul during Confession. He wrote the following prayer, called "Stay with Me, Lord":

> Stay with me, Lord, for it is necessary to have Thee present so that I do not forget Thee. Thou knowest how easily I abandon Thee.
>
> Stay with me, Lord, because I am weak, and I need Thy strength that I may not fall so often.
>
> Stay with me, Lord, for Thou art my light, and without Thee I am in darkness.
>
> Stay with me, Lord, to show me Thy will.

Stay with me, Lord, so that I hear Thy voice and follow Thee.

Stay with me, Lord, for I desire to love Thee very much and to be in Thy company always.

Stay with me, Lord, if Thou wishes me to be faithful to Thee.

Stay with me, Lord, for as poor as my soul is I want it to be a place of consolation for Thee, a nest of love.

Stay with me, Jesus, for it is getting late and the day is coming to a close, and life passes; death, judgment, eternity approaches. It is necessary to renew my strength, so that I will not stop along the way and for that, I need Thee. It is getting late and death approaches. I fear the darkness, the temptations, the dryness, the cross, the sorrows. O how I need Thee, my Jesus, in this night of exile!

Stay with me tonight, Jesus, in life with all its dangers. I need Thee.

Let me recognize Thee as Thy disciples did at the breaking of the bread, so that the Eucharistic Communion be the Light which disperses the darkness, the force which sustains me, the unique joy of my heart.

Stay with me, Lord, because at the hour of my death, I want to remain united to Thee, if not by communion, at least by grace and love.

Stay with me, Jesus, I do not ask for Divine consolation, because I do not merit it, but the gift of Thy Presence, oh yes, I ask this of Thee!

Stay with me, Lord, for it is Thou alone I look for, Thy Love, Thy Grace, Thy Will, Thy Heart, Thy Spirit because I love Thee and ask no other reward but to love Thee more and more.

With a firm love, I will love Thee with all my heart while on earth and continue to love Thee perfectly during all eternity. Amen.

When our group arrived in the small church which St. Padre Pio served, I smelled an overwhelming bouquet of roses. I asked everyone else if they could smell it, as I saw no flowers in the chapel. No one smelled the roses but me. The smell was indescribable. It was like I walked into the most fragrant gardens, full of the old-fashion roses with a sweet, lingering smell.

A priest connected to this church came up to me and asked me if I smelled roses. I said yes, and he asked me to come with him to the back of the rectory. At that time, I was introduced to Father Gino, who lived at the church and who also had the stigmata. He asked me why I came to Italy with this group at that time; I told him that I was trying to discern if God wanted me to become a Franciscan Sister. He prayed with me and informed me that God had already introduced me to my future husband and that He wanted me to be at peace with what God was going to do in my life.

The priest happened to be right. I had already met Steve, one of the kindest, most loving, and sensitive men here on earth, and he became my husband. My nickname for him is "Stevie Wonder." We have been happily married for over thirty-six years, and God blessed us with three good men. My first son, Stephen, was born the year after we got married. I was placed on total bed rest for eight months, and then he was delivered via C-section. I went into full-blown eclampsia. I was told that I should never attempt to have any other children, as my body didn't handle pregnancy well. Two and a half years later, however, my second son was born; we named him Michael, after my nine-year-old patient who died of leukemia. And four years later, my third son was born; we named him David. I had eight months of bed rest with each pregnancy.

When I was three months pregnant with Stephen, we decided we would visit our parents to announce our news. We had a dinner at my parents and gave them both a rose and a card that explained that they were going to be grandparents. They were thrilled.

I remember my father asking my mother, "What more could we ask for?"

The news of our coming child brought happy tears to our parents' eyes.

My whole family was together that day. We always had a lot of people at the dinner table. Aunts and uncles and cousins showed up and needed to eat on that particular day; there was always enough food. My mother always cooked for an army when my father was home. We never really knew who would be coming to the table.

My father would take it upon himself to go out and find someone who was homeless and hungry or in need of a shower; he would bring them home for dinner. He would point them in the direction of the showers, give them clean clothes, invite them to shave and groom themselves, and serve them dinner. We always had people at the dinner table. It didn't have to be a holiday for us to have someone we didn't know come to dinner. After we all ate together, my father would thank the stranger for joining us, offer to drive them wherever they wanted to go, and give the person anywhere from $50 to $100. He would ask them to pick themselves up, have hope, and try to get a job, and when they were in a better way, to do the same for someone else. My father paid it forward long before it became a popular saying.

My father was a captain of an oil tanker for over twenty-five years. He had both national and international licenses. One afternoon, before he left home to go back to the ship, my mother had taken a nap and had a nightmare; I heard her crying and went into her room to see if she was all right. She quietly told me that she had a dream that someone came to the door to tell her that something was wrong with Daddy. She immediately ran out into a cloud of fog and looked for him everywhere but couldn't find him. She knew that she would never see him again.

She didn't want to share what she dreamt with my father because she was afraid that something really would happen to him. I told her she needed to share it so she would be prepared if something happened when he was on the ship. I went out to my father and told him that Mom had a nightmare about losing him and that he had to speak with her about what she needs to do if anything ever happened to him while he was away on the ship. They spent the next three hours discussing everything.

Less than a week later, I received a panic call at 3:30 a.m. from my mother; she was screaming into the phone that Daddy was being transported by helicopter to St. Vincent's Hospital in New York from his oil tanker. She had received a call informing her that he was very ill and was being sent to the hospital; they might need to operate. I immediately woke up Steve; we got dressed and went to pick up Mom.

There were two St Vincent's hospitals in New York; they didn't know which one he was sent to, but we figured it out. All the way up, I prayed the Rosary and tried to reassure my mother. When we finally arrived, we jumped out of the car and went straight up to the post-op waiting room. We kept asking for his doctor to come and speak with us, as we hadn't heard anything yet. We were then asked to wait in the chapel. A priest came in to speak with us first; he said he was "terribly sorry." My father was only fifty-eight years old, and when he left home, he appeared to be in perfect health.

I then went back up to the waiting room and demanded to speak with the doctor who operated on my father. Being a nurse, I wanted to know who operated, what was found, and why he died. It was Columbus Day, a holiday, and I am painfully aware of the on-call lists at holiday time. It turned out that a gynecologist who was on call for emergency surgery had operated on my father. My father had an aneurysm in his aorta within his abdomen; it had ruptured during surgery. By the time the staff got a vascular surgeon, it was too late to save my father's life.

The hospital kept us waiting for over three hours. I felt myself getting angrier as time passed. I then called the nursing supervisor and demanded to know what happened. Why did my father die? What really happened? The nursing supervisor finally brought out an intern who was in the OR and was assigned to the case. His clothes were full of blood; he couldn't make eye contact and spoke very softly. I demanded to know what happened to my father. My mother wanted to see his body and was refused access. Something didn't sit right. Why all of this avoidance?

I don't know if it was the fact that I was pregnant, hormones, or just plain shock, but after waiting over three hours for someone to tell us what happened and the hospital sending us out an intern, I flipped out. I grabbed the intern by his scrubs and pushed him up against the wall, screaming at him that I wanted to know what happened.

How can a man leave his home so healthy and suddenly die with no explanation? Steve helped me loosen my grip on this intern's scrubs; after that, the intern just kept apologizing for my father's death, saying over and over again that it should have never happened. The supervisor finally came to the waiting room with a form allowing a full copy of my father's medical records to be sent to my mother's home. After she signed this form, we finally left for the long drive back.

Mom and I were in shock; we cried the whole way home. Steve and I stayed with her in the house so she'd have someone to talk to. She kept crying and saying how angry she was at my father.

She said, "He was supposed to die with me, not before me. He should have told God that he had to come back for me and not leave me here all alone."

Mom received telephone calls from people she had never met, from all over the world: South Africa, Korea, Japan, Sweden, France, as well as all over the United States. My father had taught many captains under his watch, from all countries. It was good to hear about their relationships. We had no idea how many lives he had touched. Because of the delay in transporting his body from New York to New Jersey, where we lived, his funeral was postponed for a week.

Hundreds of people from all over the world came to the funeral, even the owners of the oil tankers he captained. The church was absolutely packed. His crewmen carried his coffin down the long aisle in the church to the poem *O Captain, My Captain*. It was very touching to see these men crying at the loss of my father. Afterwards, our family invited everyone back to our home for refreshments. My father would have wanted it this way. People were telling stories about him and his spirit. He obviously touched many people while he lived.

It was good to hear about relationships we never knew about. People told many stories about his generosity and how he cared for his crew members and others. Dad would have been happy to be remembered with such love and devotion. Mom was like a robot as she went through the day. We were all exhausted. Later that night, my brother, who was to be married within a week from the same church where Dad had just been buried, came to my mother and suggested that he postpone their wedding.

Mom said, "Daddy loved both you and Paula, and he wouldn't want you to postpone your wedding because of his death."

So one week later, I walked down the aisle as a bridesmaid at Tommy's wedding, crying so hard because I was remembering the funeral. It was one of the toughest things I had ever done.

Daddy was quiet and gentle. He never judged anyone and had such a big heart that he was always giving of himself or helping someone in need. He allowed me to give him my first real shot during nursing school. I remember practicing giving needles on oranges one weekend. I wanted to make sure that my technique was quick and painless. He rolled up his sleeve and offered his arm as he told me stories about how as a captain, he needed to know first aid. He told me that when you are out on a ship in the middle of the ocean, there are no doctors or nurses; as the captain, he had to set broken bones and administer pain medications when emergencies occurred.

My father was proud when I graduated as an RN. He always told me how important it was for me to be self-sufficient. On my wedding day, right before we went down the aisle, he turned to me and said, "Karen, we can walk away from this whole wedding if you've changed your mind, with no problem."

I thanked him and told him how much I loved him and also how much I loved Steve. He then escorted me down the aisle and handed me over to my husband. He kissed me first and told me how much he loved me.

When Daddy died, I was three months pregnant. Our last night together, we had a large family meal. He needed a ride into Atlantic

City to catch the bus to New York so he could meet up with his ship. Steve and I took him to the bus station. We were all excited because the next time he was to be home, Tommy was going to be married. I remember hugging him and kissing him goodbye. I told him that I loved him and watched him get on the bus to New York for the last time.

After he died, everything changed in my life. My mother ran a business similar to a bed and breakfast. She was only fifty years old when my Dad died. She lived for another twenty-six years before passing away. To her, they were the hardest years of her life, because she was separated from my father.

When my father died, I completely lost it. My spiritual connection was on the brink. I was so angry with God and felt betrayed by Him. I climbed into a black hole of depression and thought I'd never come out of it. I found it hard to trust God anymore. I actually went into our church and screamed and yelled at God for taking my father so soon.

Prior to this, I felt I was able to cope with death calmly, and prayer helped immensely. But when my father died suddenly at the age of fifty-eight, I just couldn't believe that God would do this to me and my family. I cried, moaned, and walked around like a zombie. One of my aunts told me that I needed to stop grieving and help my mother through this tragic time. I couldn't do it.

Deep down inside, I knew I would see him again, but I didn't want him to be gone. I wanted to be with him; I wanted him to know that my children were going to miss getting to know him. I still needed to trust God but couldn't. My heart was closed and no longer open to God. I screamed so loudly from my grief that I couldn't hear anyone answer me. I hurt too deeply to begin to heal.

This experience taught me that God is always there, even during those times you can no longer feel His presence. He understands what it's like to lose someone you love so completely. He experiences these losses every day when someone chooses to deny Him or ignore Him in their lives. He has given us free will and only approaches us when we are open to His love. He waited patiently for me to begin the healing process. I wanted my pain at the loss of my father to be over before I brought my son into this world. Five months after burying my father, my son was born. New life brings new love, and once again, I was able to see God in my son's life.

Once again, I began to trust God.

Going Straight to Hell?

Many people are concerned about what happens when your heart stops or when you are deemed clinically dead. When I was first assigned to a cardiac unit, a patient in his forties was admitted to the unit to rule out a heart attack. The other three nurses in the unit wanted to go to lunch together. We only had four patients, so I agreed to cover the unit alone while they took their half-hour break.

When I went into the rooms to check IVs and run cardiac strips for the medical records, this young patient whistled at me and said, "I'm happy to see that the pretty nurse was assigned to me."

I smiled at him and joked, "You need to stop whistling; you are an absolute flirt." We chatted, and I told him I had noticed his religion was listed as a Catholic. "I can notify a priest to come visit you while in the hospital," I said. "Do you want that?"

He promptly said, "I'm going straight to hell; no priest would absolve me from sin because I'm one of the bad boys."

I explained to him that he didn't have much collateral circulation surrounding his heart and that he may not survive the next heart attack.

Again, he smiled and said, "When I die, I'm going straight to hell."

I told him, "No one goes to hell on my watch." I then explained that I pray for all my patients and that I would be praying for him. I pulled his bed out to the nursing station, put him on a portable monitor, and proceeded to take his blood pressure. The monitor indicated that he had gone into a cardiac arrest. The other nurses were still at lunch. I took the paddles and shocked him, with no response. I did the old method of CPR on him, mouth to mouth and compressions, but he remained without a pulse. I was so upset that I forcefully pounded on his chest and said loudly, "You will not die on my shift; in the name of Jesus, come back."

All of a sudden, he opened his eyes, and his heart rate went back to normal. After I brought his bed back into his room, he grabbed my uniform and told me that when all of this was happening, he felt like he was floating toward a white light, when all of a sudden, black tar-like figures came out of nowhere and began to pull him back down. He said he knew he was being pulled to hell. All of a sudden, he heard my voice saying, "You will not die on my shift; in the name of Jesus, come back." He then felt these black figures release his arms and legs, and he regained consciousness. He felt that Jesus had given him another chance and said, "I need to see a priest immediately."

I called the chaplain, and he came right up. The patient asked me to stand outside the curtained area, just in case he had another problem. I told him that his Confession should be confidential and that I would go back outside the room. He insisted I stand nearby.

He proceeded with his Confession and then asked me to help him with his penance. I asked him what he had in mind.

"Karen, please stay. I need you to be here," he said. He then asked me to get his wife.

When she arrived, he told her that she was the only woman he had ever truly loved. She began to cry and told him that he was going to make it and to stop worrying because they would help each other through this trying time.

He then took a large gulp and informed her that he had gone to Confession about an hour ago.

Startled, she asked, "You went to Confession? You haven't been to church since we were married."

He then told her about his out-of-body experience, and explained that he was being pulled into hell because of all the mistakes he made as a husband and father.

His wife tried to console him, saying that everyone makes mistakes and that she could forgive anything if it meant that he would live.

He then used this opportunity to tell her that he had had an affair. She quietly got up off the bed and stood at the bottom with tears in her eyes and her arms crossed. I was quietly standing by, monitoring his heart rate.

I shot him a look that clearly stated he should come clean. He picked up on my look and then told her that actually he had three affairs, but they were all over.

His wife shook as she tried to compose herself. His heart rate became irregular, and she told him she didn't want to know about these other women. She reminded him that they were married to each other and that if he was telling her about this now; it must mean that he was dying.

They talked, cried, and finally agreed that in moving forward, they would be honest; there would be no more affairs, and they would raise their children together.

By the time he left the hospital, he was reconnected with his family and God. Before he left, he called me his "angel of mercy." He thanked me for saving his life and for helping him not to go straight to hell, as he thought he would.

Eric's Story

After having my three sons, I remained in nursing to keep my skills sharp. When my second son, Michael, was around nine years old, he asked me if heroes were real. I pointed out to him that we had a cousin in the army who was currently helping out with a hero's mission. He was stationed in Africa during the great drought. Millions of people were dying of starvation, and our troops were stationed there on a peace-keeping mission. Mike and his classmates decided to adopt my cousin, Eric Kelly, as their hero and began making cards and banners for him, sending him and his troop Tastykakes, and keeping in touch every month.

Eric was so surprised to receive these notes, banners, and goodies, and he shared them with the other guys in his troop. When he finally returned home after serving in Africa, he went to the school in full uniform. He wanted to thank these kids for all the happy feelings they put into their banners, gifts, and cards and tell them that receiving these things made the troops happy and hopeful.

I remember the stressors Eric shared with me about his last deployment. He got emotional as he spoke about being "surrounded with death on all sides." He said, "No one can ever be prepared to see mothers and children, babies, dying due to lack of water and food." He said he couldn't sleep at night without seeing and hearing these people. They were screaming in pain due to starvation, and he heard the soft, high-pitched cries of babies unable to be fed.

He shared the hopelessness of the mission. He said, "I held babies the size of my hand, who were starving, and I couldn't comfort any of them."

There was not enough food, water, or help to make a dent in the devastation he had witnessed. He felt it had profoundly changed him.

As he spoke, he tried to hold his hands together so that I wouldn't see them shake. He then began to speak about how humbling it was for him to be looked at as a hero by these children, when deep down inside, he felt if he could have left this assignment, he would have. He said it made him feel hopeless and helpless inside. He had trouble coping. He said the army had been good to him, but that he needed to not reenlist again. He had two children to support.

He was married and had filed for a divorce; meanwhile, he had another baby with a woman from Germany, who kept insisting they get married. He told me that he did not intend to marry her but wanted to somehow keep his daughter in America. Life was so complicated for him because of poor choices he had made.

He wanted to send this girlfriend back to Germany and didn't want her around his daughter. He had been trying to tell her that he would arrange for her to leave but wasn't getting anywhere. He loved his daughter but didn't want to stay connected to her mother. He didn't know how to get out of this situation.

He said that in the army he made $30 per hour as a helicopter mechanic. When he applied to jobs outside the army, he was thanked for his service and offered only $7.50 or $8 per hour. At that time, there was nothing identified as post-traumatic stress syndrome; no mental health assistance was offered to him through the army.

One night, Eric went out with some high school buddies; he had a few drinks and began to say his good-byes to his friends. One of his best friends took him home, but as they spoke in the car, he never realized that this would be the last conversation they ever had. Eric said good-bye to his friend and went back to his grandmother's home, where he was staying.

When he went inside, his girlfriend from Germany began to scream at him. She followed him up the stairs to the room they slept in, screaming at him that she would be leaving him that very next day and that he would never see his daughter again once she flew back to Germany. She kept repeating that she wanted to "end our relationship."

He begged her to stop yelling at him; his grandmother was imploring the girlfriend from behind, asking her to please stop, saying, "Please, no more fighting; stop yelling at him, please."

Finally, Eric told his girlfriend that he would put an end to it all; in a split-second, before anyone could stop him, he pulled a gun from under his pillow and put it up to his head, saying he would "stop it all." He promptly shot a bullet through his head and bled out while his grandmother held his head in her lap, screaming, "No, no. Please, God, no."

No one can appreciate the unimaginable pain that is the ultimate explanation for such a tragic action. No one, therefore, can judge a person whose choice we cannot fathom, whose life we can remember but cannot restore, and whose pain we cannot understand.

The church teaches that suicide is wrong; it is contrary to the Fifth Commandment. It is an action that runs counter to the proper love of self, as well as love for God, the giver of life. We are stewards of our lives, not owners. People who take their own life also wrong others; those who remain experience loss, bewilderment, and grief. You won't find anything in that teaching about going to hell. Pity, not condemnation, is the response of the church.

Prayers are offered for the deceased. The deceased's life is still celebrated. Burial with dignity, in consecrated ground, is provided for people who die this way. Not that long ago, Christian burial was denied to those who took their own lives. There may have been another denial at work in those days, too: denial of our inability to understand the pain.

We assumed that those who chose to take their own lives were acting freely and under no psychological distress or illness. Or worse, there may have been a denial of responsibility to try to understand the pain.

So for those of us who remain, the church encourages paying attention to the pain that produced the action. Then look forward, not back, to pain within ourselves and pain in others, especially when we see no signs and hear no calls for help. Why do we avoid speaking to one another about inner pain? Why are we not more sensitive to the pain in others' hearts or read the pain in their eyes? Why do we spend millions for pain relief over the counter or by prescription, but not spend the time it takes to encourage those who may be hurting to open up?

This kind of thinking is all now part of the church's pastoral response to the tragedy of suicide. It seems to me that there has to be some mysterious insulation enveloping those who commit suicide. Tragically, their minds cannot be read by those around them, nor can they reach out and ask for help. The church teaches through liturgy and, on occasions like these, stresses God's divine mercy.

Take a look at Psalm 103 and recall the dimensions of God's mercy: as far as the east is from the west, as high as the skies are above the earth. The church still teaches that there is a hell but leaves it to God to decide who should go there. And divine decisions, in this regard, are filtered through divine mercy. Tragedy at the end of this life is no sure sign of an eternal tragedy in the next.

Approximately seventeen years later, out of the clear blue sky, I received a telephone call from a young woman. She identified herself as Eric's daughter and told me that her uncle said I could help her. Her mother threw her out of the house, at seventeen. She had been staying at the boyfriend's home and then on various couches or sleeping in her car. She couldn't go back home.

Her mother had never formally told her that Eric was her father. Shortly after his death, her mother married Eric's stepbrother, to stay in America. When she was seventeen, her mother threw her out of their home and then threw her father's dog tags at her. She angrily informed her that the father she thought to be her own was not her real father, and Eric's daughter then asked me if she could come over to talk and learn about her father's family. I said yes, and she came that night. She did not know anything about her father. Her mother became very unbalanced emotionally and kept insisting she go to a homeless shelter and that this would teach her a hard lesson.

Eric was obviously irrational when he killed himself. He hadn't planned this ahead of time, didn't leave a note, and never expected to kill himself that night. When I took his daughter to the cemetery, she laid down on top of his grave and cried. She kept asking me why. She then said that she couldn't help but wonder how different her life would have been if he had lived and her mother hadn't been so abusive with her.

That day, we asked Eric's daughter to move into our home so she could experience what her father was like based on pictures, stories, and old home movies. She looked so much like him: same ears, same smile. She had his walk and folded her arms just like her dad did. We felt God sent her to us so she could heal by connecting with her father's family.

Suicide as sudden death is tragic and leaves many broken when it takes place. I thank God that the army now recognizes post-traumatic stress, because back then, no one knew what happened, and there was no counseling offered to those who served.

My Experience with Jesus

I know from my own experiences that God is real and that there is life after death. Death is not the end. When I was forty-two, I was working as the administrator in a nursing home. I began to experience double and triple vision. I had chronic fatigue, had choking episodes, and was finding it hard to function. I went to my physician, and he proceeded to test me for everything under the sun. Everything was coming back normal. It got so bad that I couldn't get out of bed. I had no idea what was wrong with me, as I am normally the type of person who can work through anything. I felt very frustrated with myself. Normal light shining through the window hurt my eyes. A regular clock ticking sounded like a bomb going off in my head. The covers placed over me while in bed hurt my skin and felt like nails leaning on my body. I wore dark black wraparound sunglasses in a dark room with black curtains, and my eyes still hurt.

I stayed home for over two weeks and remained in bed this entire time, without knowing what was wrong. My mother came over every morning to help Steve get the kids ready for school. She would bring me tea, breakfast, and snacks to eat, but I kept choking whenever I ate or drank anything. One day, she asked if I was depressed about anything. I answered no, except for not being able to lift my head off the pillow. I was frustrated that my symptoms were real, but none of the tests led to any conclusions.

My eyes hurt whenever I saw light, so my room was kept dark. I was one sick girl. Even though I was an RN, I couldn't figure out what my diagnosis was. I laid in bed every day, asking God to help me figure out what was wrong. I had little to no muscle strength. I would try to hold up my head with my hand, but by the end of each day, this no longer worked. I found myself praying and sleeping a lot.

My doctor was stumped; he didn't know what to test next. After two weeks of feeling sorry for myself, I decided to go back to work. I thought, maybe if I pushed myself, I would feel better. I pulled myself together and drove myself to work at the nursing home. I began to make rounds to see my senior residents and found myself holding onto the handrails. I slowly walked back to my office and returned to my desk, where I promptly passed out. The noise from falling over onto my desk alerted the staff in the next room.

When I came to, the staff was making plans to call 911. I asked them to call Steve, who took me to a hospital closer to my home. They gave us the name of Dr. Scott Tzorfas, a neurologist who was new in the area. He asked Steve to bring me right over to his office.

We arrived at the neurologist's office, and the doctor had me climb up onto his exam table; he asked me to follow his finger, which I tried to do, with little success. As I tried to follow his finger, I fell over onto the table and couldn't get back up on my own.

He said, "The good news is that you don't have a brain tumor or Lou Gehrig's disease. The bad news is that you have myasthenia gravis, a neuromuscular disease, which is an autoimmune disease. You need to be hospitalized immediately."

I didn't want to hear this. I was in complete denial. I told Steve that I didn't have time to be sick (as if I had a choice) and that we needed to go home immediately. I told the neurologist that he was nuts and that he couldn't diagnosis me that fast with no tests. I kept telling Steve to leave, while the neurologist began explaining what to do if I had a respiratory arrest that night. He strongly suggested that I go to the hospital before my lungs crashed.

I told Dr. Tzorfas that I had three sons who needed their mommy; also, I still needed to do the Christmas shopping, decorate the tree, and get things ready for the holiday.

My husband was in shock. I didn't want Steve to hear what Dr. Tzorfas said. I told the doctor that he should stop scaring my husband.

I told him I would go home and rest for the next week and that I would come back feeling better. I was determined to prove to the neurologist that he was wrong. Nurses are such tough patients; we think we know it all. In many cases, we do know what to expect next, but in this case, I was caught off guard. I was too close to this situation to know what was happening. Like my husband, I was in shock too.

The only thing I remembered from nursing school about myasthenia gravis (MG) was that the name meant "muscle death." We left after Steve promised to call Dr. Tzorfas if anything became worse. We didn't say a word to each other all the way home. I quietly cried and kept wiping tears from my cheeks, hoping that Steve wouldn't see how upset I was. When we got home, I asked him to leave me alone. I went straight to my computer to look up the symptoms for this disease. I saw pictures of patients who had their muscles drop as the day went on. I cried and pleaded with God to make it go away. I told Him that I would be much more useful to Him if I was spared this disease.

Steve knocked quietly on the door to ask if I was all right. I told him that I wanted to be alone. I began to pace and pictured Jesus standing right in front of me. I kept asking Him, "Why?" I remember giving Him all of the reasons that I didn't have time to be this sick. I even yelled and screamed at God while pacing back and forth. I did not want this to be true. I was very concerned for my children and my husband. How was this going to play out? I listed everything that I had to do in this life, all my plans, from getting the laundry done to decorating the house for Christmas, to buying the kids presents, to planning events as the boys grew up, to progressing in my own business, to paying the bills, to living to see my own grandchildren. Everything crashed in on me. I felt so helpless, so vulnerable, so scattered.

The only thing I could equate this helpless feeling to was my experiences with patients who discover they have cancer or a rare disease. Imagine you are well one day and have minor symptoms and go for a checkup and are told you are dying. That was how I felt. I felt like I had been flattened by a giant bowling ball. I was also concerned about my lack of control in my own life. I was beginning to understand, right from the start of my illness, what it was like to have your life completely out of control.

I argued with God and reminded Him that I was an RN and a counselor, and I helped other people through a healing ministry. I told Him that I would do anything to avoid suffering with this disease for the rest of my life. I think I proposed many ways He could spin this, other than a definite diagnosis of myasthenia gravis. I was like a lawyer giving testimony to a judge in court, except the case was my life and how the rest of it should be played out.

When I calmed down, I heard God speak softly to me. He said, "You need to experience what it is like to be in a body that doesn't work in order to do My will."

I told him that I needed to be assured that He would be with me every step of the way; if I felt sure of this, then I would completely surrender to His will.

I felt God's arms around me, hugging me tightly. I knew I would learn from this experience and be able to handle things if He was with me through it all. I stopped pacing and felt very peaceful and began to accept this. I finally said yes.

I was so weak that by the time I opened the door and Steve came in, I felt like a damp, worn-out wash rag. He held me in his arms, and I sobbed loudly. He told me, "We're going to get through this illness together."

Even though I knew that this was something God wanted me to experience, it didn't make it any easier to deal with. I was so humbled as a caregiver and registered nurse to let others take care of me: my husband, my children, and my household.

During that week, I slept in a dark room because my eyes still hurt whenever any light was present. I remember the long hours of lying there, thinking how I could explain to my sons why Mommy was lying in bed all the time. I asked Steve to find information on myasthenia gravis that was easily understood; I had him print it out and then asked my oldest son, Stephen, to read it to me one night. Stephen was in seventh grade at that time and was into computers at an early age.

He brought down his flashlight and pointed it at the paper and began to read out loud about my illness. With each line he read, he had many questions. He was showing me clearly that he understood this disease and wanted to help me with it. He then asked me the question I dreaded the most:

"Mommy, are you dying?"

I gulped, took a deep breath, and tried to answer him as best as I could.

I didn't know yet what was going to happen, but I told him that I wasn't dying but that I needed him to help Daddy with the other boys more because Mommy couldn't help anymore at this time.

He promised me that he would argue less and make sure he helped his dad get his brothers ready for school.

By making Stephen read out loud to me, I knew he would begin to comprehend the scope of what was happening and wouldn't be afraid of asking questions. He knew that the covers hurt my skin because of the hypersensitivity. We discussed the possibility of me being put on a ventilator. He was always straightforward and concrete, but he asked how we were going to communicate if I was ever put on a machine for breathing. We decided that night that if I was unable to speak, we would hold one another's hand and squeeze it three times for the words "I love you."

The next night, I had Steve send Michael down to see me; he was two and a half years younger than Stephen. He was so cute and expressive at times. He was also very sensitive to people who had problems. He was the child to bring someone home to eat or help defend someone being picked on at school.

Mike had a friend who lived across the street whose mother had Multiple Sclerosis. While I was laying there, not knowing if I was going to live or die, Mike came in from playing to speak to me about his friend. He told me that he thought his friend's mommy was "sicker than me and wanted to know if his mommy died, could we adopt him." He explained to me that he "really wouldn't take up much room"; he would share his bed with him and told me that he didn't eat much.

I told him that Daddy and I would have to see how things go and then explained that the doctor wanted me to go into the hospital for some tests because Mommy wasn't feeling strong anymore. I could see his mind racing with questions.

Some of Mike's questions were, "Who is this doctor, Mommy? Why does he need you to go to a hospital? Doesn't he know we need you here? Daddy doesn't do things like you do; he tries, but it's not the same. Can we come and visit you there? How long will you be sick? Can't they give you medicine?"

I could tell that Mike was very anxious about this situation and asked Steve to call the school to inform his teacher and counselors about our home situation, so they could help him with this anxiety.

While I was in the hospital in isolation, I found out that Mike's friend's mother did die and that he had to move in with his father after the funeral. This made Mike very anxious.

My children feared that I could die from this disease, and this caused them to experience much anxiety and depression. I couldn't fix this situation. I was usually the one they spoke to about situations that made them anxious, but my illness was the cause of their anxiety. Their dad was there for them but was very quiet; he found it hard to talk with them about my health. They knew I was going to be in the hospital longer than expected because of the seriousness of my illness. Steve would tell them that everything was going to be all right.

My sons were used to me hugging and kissing them. Before they went out the door in the morning, I would lay hands on each of them and pray over them in tongues. They thought every mother did this (they also thought I prayed in Spanish; I found this out many years later). At night before they went to bed, I would put the sign of the cross on their forehead and pray once again for each of them, for their protection, for their growth in the Spirit, for them to have good God-filled lives and turn out to be good men.

Our youngest son, David, was only five years old when I became so sick. He would come with the dog and lay right beside me. He was very quiet around me; he didn't say much except how much he missed playing with me and missed my hugs and kisses. He did tell me daily how much he loved me.

My mother came every day to help. David told me that he loved

Nanny but she didn't have the same smell as me. He liked playing with the flashlight in my room, right next to my bed. He took comfort at sitting next to my bed, at the bottom of the bed, or on the side so he could hear my voice. I was trying to soak up as much of the kids as possible because I really didn't know if I was ever going to see them again. I found myself missing them so much, even though I hadn't even gone to the hospital yet.

All three boys were worried about Christmas. They kept asking me if I would be home in time. They asked who would make the cookies for Santa and help decorate the house and tree if I wasn't here. I told them Daddy would do this, and they said he could help decorate, but they didn't think he knew how to make cookies. I told them they didn't have to worry, that between their grandparents, aunts, and my sister, they would have plenty of cookies for Santa and for them.

That first week, I asked Steve to let my mother help with cooking, cleaning, and doing the laundry. He said he wanted to do the laundry. When I asked why, he told me that he needed to feel like he had control of something. I certainly understood.

I remember one day my mother came down to my bedroom and asked me how she could help. She was brushing my hair with her hand and kneeling beside my bed. I began to cry. She asked me why I never smiled anymore.

I told her, "Mom, I am smiling; the muscles in my face don't work right, so you can't see it, but I am smiling."

She had that same look as when she spoke about my cousins dying. I saw her really try her best with the boys and Steve. She was overwhelmed with everything going on. I felt she was mourning my loss before I had even died.

A week later, after resting in bed, I readied myself to go see Dr. Tzorfas, my neurologist. I thought I looked better. I still held on to the hope that God had changed His mind and this was just a bad flu. It didn't happen. Dr. Tzorfas took us in just as we arrived. I sat on the exam table, confident that I was not doing badly. He raised his hand and asked me to follow his finger. As soon as I tried to focus my eyes on his finger, I fell back onto the exam table. All my muscles dropped, and I had very little strength.

He told me that I was much worse and needed to get right over to the hospital. I told him I couldn't go into the hospital without explaining to my sons that Mommy wouldn't be around for some time. Stephen was eleven, Mike was nine, and David was only five. I promised him that as soon as I spoke to my family, I would come to the hospital. He told me that if I didn't meet him in the hospital by eight o'clock that night, he would personally drive down, put me in his car, and bring me there himself. Then he told me that I had a very serious and dangerous condition.

After I went home and spoke with the boys separately, I collected my pillow, toiletries, and Bible and went to the hospital. I was admitted and put into an isolation room for my own good, as my immune system was attacking itself. I didn't have the strength to fight any other infections.

That night, Dr. Tzorfas did what he called a Tensilon test, which would prove whether I had myasthenia gravis or not. He told me that if the test was positive, I would feel like superwoman for several minutes; all my muscles would lift once he injected the medication, which they did. After feeling like a worn-out rag doll for so long, it felt so good. Then after about a minute or two, all my muscles suddenly dropped (he neglected to tell me about this after-effect of the test). I crashed.

That night, I stayed in isolation. Steve took down the clock in the room, since the ticking noise was like a bomb going off in my head. The room was made as dark as possible. The staff was told to check on me hourly throughout the night, as I was very weak (they were afraid I couldn't ring for them if I needed someone). I was located right next to the desk areas for close observation; both doors to the isolation room were shut so things could be quieter. Steve stayed as late as he could; I remember telling him to go home and get some rest. He looked exhausted.

After he left, I tried to go to sleep but couldn't, so I prayed. As the night went on, I realized that the night shift nurse had stopped coming in to check on me. When I went to call her with the button, I had no strength to push it. I suddenly realized that my legs, body, and arms, as well as my head, were like lead. I had no ability to call for anyone. I remember thinking that this must be a precursor to dying. I was in a panic, thinking that I wouldn't see my husband and sons again. My mind was still fully functioning; my eyes could still blink, but my voice was weak. No one could hear my calls because of how weak my voice was.

I remember thinking that the nurse assumed I was sleeping, but I was fully awake, even though I was not moving. I panicked and asked God to help me sleep. I thought if I fell asleep, death wouldn't be too painful for me. I'd just stop breathing. As I lay there praying, tears dropped down my cheeks onto the sheets under me. I asked God again to help me. Suddenly, I saw a being out of the corner of my eye; she was floating toward me, and the closer she came, the bigger she got. She was full of bright white light, and when she came toward me, I felt sudden warmth all over.

This being whispered into my ear, "Relax, you are going to be fine. God is with you."

She was holding a bubble-like flower, similar to a dandelion before it flowers. She blew on the flower, and tiny angels came out of it and began to gather at my feet. They whirled around my body and caused the heaviness in my muscles to dissipate. I felt warmth and healing. She explained that they were going to help relax me. She added that I should not worry; I was not going to die but was going to be put to sleep. Before I knew it, I fell asleep. I can't remember having such a relaxing sleep, ever before or since. Every muscle in my body was aching prior to this. I didn't know if I dreamed it, but it didn't seem like a dream.

I remember asking her what her name was, and she laughed. She said, "Karen, don't you remember me? It's Patty!"

My cousin Patty had died several years earlier of leukemia. She was young and had two children at the time. We were born two weeks apart and were like sisters growing up. I was so happy that God sent me my cousin to help me through this night.

That next morning, I remember I awoke to a frantic RN talking to herself. The lights were put on, and she said, "Mrs. Stratoti, please forgive me. I thought you were asleep all night. I checked on you through the double doors and didn't see you move at all, so I assumed you were sleeping."

She panicked when she saw that I was unable to respond other than moving my eyes. She explained that she had never taken care of someone with my disease before and said she was going to get some Mestinon and would be right back. Mestinon was the drug used to help increase my muscle strength, and it does work fast. She begged me not to tell the doctor.

After she injected my IV with the medication, I immediately felt my muscles lift. She kept apologizing, and I asked her if she was on the next night. She said she was, and I told her that I would give an in-service on myasthenia gravis disease; I wanted everyone who would be caring for me to attend.

The muscles involved in my situation were eyelid movement, facial expression, chewing, talking and swallowing. At times, I also had problems with my neck and limb movements. I had weakness of all muscles, difficulty swallowing, slurred speech, blurred and double vision, was unstable in my gait, had weakness in my arms, hands, fingers, legs, and neck and, together with shortness of breath and impaired speech, I was a mess.

My severity of weakness fluctuated during the day, usually being least severe in the morning and worse as the day progressed. There were times that I couldn't even hold my head up with my hand. I literally had to lie flat in bed.

I called Steve and shared with him what happened throughout that night; I then asked him to print out twenty copies of the handout on myasthenia gravis and bring them for the in-service. I had a packed room that night. I explained what had happened and educated everyone from the head nurse to the housekeeper about my disease. Even the transportation aides came to this in-service. I asked them to leave a handout at the nurses' station for the day shift and to put one of them into my medical record.

I am sure that everyone appreciated my information on MG.

My neurologist got a kick out of what I did. I explained to him that moving forward, I needed to have Mestinon pills at my bedside, in case my muscles begin to drop; he understood and wrote the order. The supervisor came into my room to inform me that they didn't allow pills at the bedside. I asked why, and she said it wasn't in their policy to do such a thing. I told her I wanted to discuss their policy with their director of nursing.

The director came into the room, and to my surprise, I knew him. When I first met him, he was an orderly at another hospital where I had worked. We discussed what had happened, and he directed the staff to change the policy and follow the physician's order. I felt calmer after this occurred.

For the next seven months, I was in and out of the hospital many times. I spent most of the time either getting testing done or waiting for the results of the tests. I was always in a private room, and so I would pray and listen to my CDs while meditating. It was not unusual for me to open my eyes after meditating to find nurses, aides, and physicians sitting at the bottom of my bed, meditating themselves or relaxing while waiting for me to open my eyes. I came to know the staff so well that many of them would start their days by asking me to remember them in my prayers or remember a special intention of theirs.

After I tried for many months to get stronger, and doing a process called plasmapheresis, we realized that nothing was getting me stronger.

Plasmapheresis is a procedure in which abnormal antibodies are removed from the blood and high-dose intravenous immune globulin is put into your system to temporarily modify the immune system and add antibodies from donated blood. This was a hard thing to do daily. I had to lay on a gurney with both arms outstretched, IVs in both arms, as they flushed out the immune system.

I remember lying there, praying that every breath I took would be a prayer to God, every blink of my eye would become a prayer; every fiber of my being would be used to give God glory. This offering of my body, mind, and spirit was the only way I could cope with what was happening to me.

I remember sometimes I used to lie there six or seven hours at a time. In order to get through the day, I began to visualize what it must have been like for Jesus to have hung on the Cross for as long as He did before finally dying.

After several months trying plasmapheresis, we concluded that it wasn't working. Dr. Tzorfas said he thought I should have a thymectomy (removal of the thymus gland). He felt it would slow down the progress of this disease. The Myasthenia Gravis Foundation of America (www. myasthenia.org) defines a thymectomy as the surgical removal of the thymus gland, which plays a major role in the development of the body's immune system and has been demonstrated to play a role in the development of MG. It is removed to combat the weakness caused by MG.

I felt very humbled and weak with this condition. Nothing I had done so far was working to get my body stronger. I felt that suffering had no value in this case. Alla Bozarth-Cambell once said, "It is the use that one makes of suffering, through attitude and action, that can have value … Living through desperation and despair with courage and honesty can prepare us to be more understanding of and compassionate towards ourselves and others … Above all, through loss experiences we can teach ourselves a new kind of joy, one which is large enough to contain our pain and to transform it into a new kind of power, the power to make us whole."

I have learned many things while being in a body that does not work right; many people have an illness or disease that affects their daily lives, but it cannot be seen by others. In other words, you can't judge a book by its cover. People would make comments to me that showed me they didn't understand. Sometimes, I felt that I was surrounded by a fog. I could feel nothingness. I felt despair at times and then would once again feel God's presence.

Many of my daily symptoms (muscle weakness, inability to swallow, and eyes looking like my lids were almost closed) could not be seen by the person I was dealing with. People would pass judgment on my needing an electric wheelchair while shopping. One person pointed at me and asked loudly, "She's too young to be in that wheelchair; what's wrong with her?"

People tend to understand what can be seen as a clear disability rather than accept that fact that you may have a muscle disease, or a heart condition, or some other internal disease.

Life is too short to hold anything against another human being. It takes too much energy to not forgive or hold something in anger against someone else. Forgiveness is much better and healthier. Life is too unclear to judge the actions of others; time is better spent in trying to understand your own motives. Life is too precious to not share it with others. When you give to others, it tends to come back to you in ways you could never even begin to imagine.

Henri J.M. Nouwen, in his book *Out of Solitude*, said, "We feel quite uncomfortable with an invitation to enter into someone's pain before doing something about it … Still when we honestly ask ourselves which persons in our lives mean most to us, we often find that it is those, who, instead of giving much advice, solutions, or cures, have chosen rather to share our pain and touch our wounds with a gentle and tender hand."

Leo Buscaglia, in *The Courage of Conviction*, said, "I believe that life was meant to be experienced in joy, love, and tranquility, and any deviation from this is due to personal maladjustment. We must not fear anxiety, pain, confusion, or despair, providing that they serve as symptoms of a life out of balance, and therefore provide an incentive to find new ways to move to happiness and a celebration of life."

Jesus Chose My Surgeon

Steve and I prayed for guidance on which surgeon should do this much-needed surgery. I checked around the hospital to see what surgeon had the best report card on infection control. I asked my fellow nurses, "If it was your surgery, who would you go to?" Hands down, I was told to choose Dr. Fred Weber, a thoracic surgeon. Everyone warned me that although he was an excellent surgeon, he had a miserable bedside manner.

I made an appointment with Dr. Weber. Steve and I went to discuss the fact that I needed a thymectomy. He looked like a younger Santa Claus with a dark handlebar mustache.

When I told him that we had prayed about who should do my surgery, he stopped me and asked, "Who put you up to this? This is a joke, right?"

I said clearly, "This is no joke," told him that I was in need of a thymectomy, and added that we had picked him to do my surgery.

He then asked my husband, "Is she for real?"

Steve answered that of course I was for real and added, "We have been praying about this for several months in the event that surgery was necessary."

I was not getting any better doing the plasmapheresis, and we were told by the neurologist that this was the next step to stop the progression of this disease.

Dr. Weber then said he doubted very much that our insurance would cover this surgery, so I asked him to call the insurance company in front of us. I assured him that for the last eight months, we tried everything suggested, and this was what we were told needed to be done. When he called the insurance company, they immediately granted him permission to do this surgery. He was shocked, for he had anticipated trouble.

He then admitted to me that he hadn't done this type of surgery on anyone with myasthenia gravis before and explained that a thymectomy involved cutting through my chest wall and ribs to remove the thymus gland. Being a thoracic surgeon, he'd done open heart surgeries but never removed a thymus gland, which stretches over the heart area.

After sharing with him all the prayer that had been offered and testing we had been put through, he realized that we were not playing a joke on him. He asked me and Steve to come into his back office.

He told me that never in his career had anyone come into his office to say they had prayed about who should do their surgery. He appeared nervous for a while, until I told him that I had been praying daily for everyone involved in my care, and that he need not worry about the surgery, if he promised me one thing.

He asked what, and I said, "You are to be an empty vessel operating on me, as Jesus will be the surgeon."

He was absolutely blown away. I could tell that this was unparalleled in his experience. I apologized for being so blunt but explained that the surgery needed to be done by him because, for whatever reason, "Jesus chose him to do this surgery."

He told me that he wanted to show me something and opened up several bookcases that were covered on his walls. These bookcases contained old versions of the Bible. He then informed me that he was once a monk and took his studies seriously. He left the order and got married, left the Catholic church, and joined the Lutheran church. He had thought some other physician sent me into his office to mock his studies, as they knew he had been in a monastery.

I assured him that this was for real; I also requested that we pray together prior to surgery and that he put the Gregorian chant on the speakers while operating. He was delighted. He claimed that the nurses always insisted on playing the oldies. He would be delighted to tell them that I requested this holy music. I was finally ready for this surgery and after fully discussing it with Steve, we scheduled it.

On a scale of 1-10, 10 being the highest pain level, the anesthesiologist informed me I would be at 20. My chest cavity would be pulled apart, similar to open heart surgery, and they would use titanium to wire the chest and ribs together after removing my thymus. When I awakened, I would be on a ventilator; no one could say how long I would be on the ventilator. Throughout the preparation for surgery, the surgery itself, and the aftermath, I had one of the most moving and blessed experiences of my life.

Meeting with Jesus

The night prior to my surgery, my mother brought in some of her prayer buddies to pray over me. One woman in this group had gone on a pilgrimage to San Giovanni Rotondo, a monastery in Foggia, Italy. She brought with her a relic of St. Padre Pio, which was one of the gloves he wore during Mass. Padre Pio was asked to intercede during my surgery; the ladies placed this holy relic on my chest, and during their prayers, I smelled roses. I did not know much about Padre Pio except that he had received the stigmata on September 20, 1918, which he bore for the rest of his life; this included the five wounds of Christ. He possessed the following gifts: bilocation, celestial perfume, the reading of hearts, miraculous cures, remarkable conversions, and prophetic insight. I felt honored that they were able to do this prior to surgery and felt more prepared.

After surgery, and several days in post-ICU, I felt just as weak as prior to surgery. I saw my primary care physician, Dr. Gall, and asked him to do a complete blood count for me. He said, "Stop being a nurse and just be my patient." I disagreed with this remark and told him something was wrong. I still "had no energy," and "it hurt to breathe." He ordered the bloodwork.

About an hour later, the results came back, and we discovered that my hemoglobin was a 3; it should have been between 12 and 15. I had severe shortness of breath, heart palpitations, and chest pain, which all made sense, as my body was unable to get enough oxygen due to my loss of blood. Dr. Gall apologized and informed me that I needed blood as soon as possible.

I was happy and relieved that they had found the problem. They immediately transferred me back to the ICU. The RN who was assigned to me was very young and looked inexperienced. I remember jokingly reminding her to check my blood type against the bag of blood and to read to me the patient ID number to make sure she was giving the right blood to the right patient. She followed all the procedures while hanging the first bag of blood. After about two hours, I began to breathe better, had less chest pain, and actually sat up on the side of the bed and ate something. I felt like my muscles were working much better. I remember feeling somewhat closer to normal.

About four hours into this first transfusion, Steve was looking less worried, and my dear friend, Sr. Judy, was talking with me when my mother walked in to visit. I seemed to have more strength, and my cheeks looked rosier, according to Mom. I remember saying that the worst was over and that the bag of blood I just received made me feel so much stronger.

When the nurse came in to hang the second bag of blood, she brought two bags in with her, but I was feeling stronger and didn't notice that she had hung one of the bags of blood and left the room. This time, I was given the wrong blood type and immediately went into anaphylactic shock. The immune system never rests—its cells constantly patrol the circulation. Without the immune system, the body would be overwhelmed with infections. With it, blood transfusions must be performed with great care. If incompatible blood is given in a transfusion, the donor cells are treated as if they were foreign invaders, and the patient's immune system attacks them accordingly. Not only is the blood transfusion rendered useless, but a potentially massive activation of the immune system can cause shock, kidney failure, circulatory collapse, and death.

I coded within seconds of receiving the wrong type of blood. I felt like a rag that someone had twisted into a knot. Being an RN myself, I realized what the problem was. I began to convulse, I became short of breath, and my muscles began to tighten. I felt like my heart was going to come right out of my chest, and I could barely speak. I tried to tell

Steve to stop the blood but couldn't; however, the look on my face and my convulsions made him start screaming for the nurse right away.

About a minute later, it felt like ice-cold water was entering my veins. I began to shiver and shake and realized that my jaw was locked. Suddenly, my spirit rose out of my body, and I felt no pain. I heard the staff calling a code to my hospital room. The last thing I remembered was hearing Steve scream for the nurses to come quick.

At this point, I no longer heard any familiar voices. I felt no pain but seemed to float and was as light as a feather. I had no body to contain me. I heard a humming and then a peaceful silence. I felt like I was slowly floating up a well-lit street. I was completely enveloped in God's unconditional love and warmth and light. I had no more anxiety and no more worries. My spirit was flying through a tunnel. I remember seeing golden homes and castles, whole communities, all types of dwellings that glistened like stars. It is so difficult to describe but unforgettable. I was in awe of the beautiful sights. I heard angelic voices softly singing; I had never heard anything like it on earth. I felt like I was on a magic carpet riding through the center of the city. Gold and silver, jewels in various brilliant colors, and diamonds were all sparkling along the pathway. It was overwhelming and breathtaking.

I feel unable to put into words what I personally experienced. Upon my arrival to what I thought was heaven, I floated effortlessly into the lap of my precious Jesus. My eyes went down. I felt so humbled; my tears started to flow, and then He ever so gently lifted my head by placing His hand under my chin. I had no fear and felt only warmth and love. He looked as I always pictured him. I will describe Him here as my "Beach Bum Jesus": He had dark skin and soft blue-green eyes, His hair was long and free flowing, and He wore a brilliant white shroud. He appeared to be sitting on a cloud in the shape of a throne. I felt extremely peaceful.

The humming sounds were angels singing in adoration and praise to the Lord. I began to cry. I couldn't help myself; I had been through a lot of pain and suffering this year and gave it all up to God. I felt like I was home. I felt like I could take a deep breath again. However, I instinctively knew that I would see Steve and my sons again.

Jesus spoke to me in my mind. He asked me, very softly, "Why are you crying?"

My answer to Him was that I felt I had failed Him. You see, during my entire hospital experiences over that last year, I prayed throughout each day to give myself to God, body, mind, and spirit.

Because I was so weak, I prayed that every breath I took be a prayer to God, every beat of my heart be a prayer to God, and every blink of my eyes be a prayer to God.

At the same time, I remember thinking that my body had failed Him in some way.

He gently lifted my face, looked right into my soul, and said, "You haven't failed me. I am so happy with your prayer and how you surrendered to Me through your suffering."

I felt as light as a feather when he lifted me up by touching my chin. He motioned with His hand, and right before my eyes, I suddenly saw my father, Thomas Joseph Cassidy, who had been dead for over fourteen years, and my father-in-law, Dominick Stratoti, who had been dead for over two years. Both were smiling at me and appeared to be happy.

Behind them, I saw my grandparents, who had passed, and other family members who had passed. But my father and father-in-law were out front. They both looked much younger than I remembered and very strong. They were very excited to see me and both wore tool belts around their waist.

As they hugged me and greeted me, I remember my father saying, "Honey, you have to go back; we aren't ready with your home yet."

I remember saying, "I'm never leaving heaven; I was in a body that failed me and feel so wholly alive right here. No more pain, no more suffering, no more fear. I am home."

I never wanted to leave, because I knew that this was where I ultimately belonged.

I kept turning to Jesus and asking Him, "This is heaven, right?"

He smiled and escorted me to the next group of people waiting for me. Jesus had such a sense of humor, and I loved watching Him smile at me. I felt that I was walking with my closest friend. He answered all my questions as soon as I formed them. It was a neat exchange.

He then brought me before a crowd of souls I did not recognize. As far as the eye could see, they were lined up to greet me.

I saw thousands and thousands of souls; I didn't understand what was happening. I asked Jesus, "Who are all these souls?"

He said, "Do you remember the prayer you said daily for the souls who had died and who have no one else on earth to pray for them? Well, these are all those souls. You asked Me for divine mercy on these souls, and I granted this request. They have come to greet you and to thank you."

I was so overwhelmed and absolutely speechless.

I recognized one voice that I heard. I wasn't sure who it was, but somehow, I knew this person. When I was an administrator in a nursing home, we accepted a man named Bobby as a resident. He was placed in an orphanage after being born very deformed. When we accepted Bobby as a resident, my staff and I realized that he would be hard to deal with because of his inability to speak or communicate. He was the size of an eight-year-old and reminded us all of an innocent boy. I never heard Bobby's voice on earth, but we did have a unique connection. I understood whatever he was trying to say. When he was having a bad day, my staff would bring him into my office, and we would "talk."

Prior to his death, I actually made him a badge that had his full name on it with the title "Assistant to the Administrator." Part of his "job" was to meet me in the morning and carry my briefcase into my office. He was so precious. My staff and I fell in love with this young man. He was in a wheelchair, was incontinent, and had to be fed by staff, but we loved him immensely. When Bobby died, we prayed for him and felt a great loss. It is not every day that you get to take care of one of God's special ones.

Well, his was the voice I recognized when I heard my name called. I remember shouting, "Bobby, is that you?"

He broke through the crowd, and I hugged him and kept asking him how he was.

He said, "Look, I am whole." He raised his arms and legs, and I saw he was completely healed. He told me how happy he was and explained that in heaven, there were no deformities.

I kept saying "Oh, my God," throughout this entire experience. I asked Jesus again if this was heaven because it felt like it to me. He smiled and then asked me to go for a walk in His garden.

Jesus raised His hand, and I saw the most beautiful garden I could ever imagine. The entrance was surrounded by an archway of bright-red roses. Now, I am not talking about the kind of roses we buy today. The roses I saw and smelled were enormous, were gorgeous, and felt velvety to touch. These roses were more beautiful than any flower I have ever seen on earth. We entered the garden through this beautiful archway of roses, brilliant in color and smell. The fragrance was familiar to me. It reminded me of the scent I often smelled when I prayed, but my description of these flowers is inadequate.

We then began to walk together on a beautiful pathway made of flat stones. The grass was greener than I had ever seen. Every blade was a different shade of vibrant green, with the glow of life within it. The trees had a glow around each leaf, and they were bent over and bowing in adoration to Jesus as we walked. The brilliantly colored flowers were also bowing in adoration. Each living petal and leaf had an effervescent glow. Small animals, beautifully colored birds, squirrels, and rabbits stopped to bow in adoration. It was breathtakingly beautiful.

Jesus asked me to tell Him my story. He said He wanted to know everything about my illness, my family concerns, and my sufferings.

I asked, "Why do I need to share all of this with You? You already know everything."

Jesus replied, "You need to know that I heard your situation."

So we sat by a lake, surrounded by beautiful plants, flowers, animals, and trees, while I told him my story. He listened attentively.

Finally, after I spent hours explaining to Him what I had suffered and my situation on earth, He asked if we could go sit beside another lake.

After enjoying this peaceful place, Jesus asked me, "Karen, would you consider doing Me a favor?"

I remember saying, "Whatever You want me to do, I will do. I am at Your service after all You have done for me."

He then asked me to consider going back to my earthly body. I was flooded with emotions and couldn't believe that He was asking me to do this.

I remember saying, "What, are You crazy? Didn't You hear a word I just said?" I then apologized, calmed down, and asked, "Do You remember what it was like to die on the cross?"

Jesus said, "Yes, I do."

I then asked Him if He remembered what it was like to have His mother watch Him die and the helplessness of not being able to do anything.

He said He remembered what it was like to see His own mother, Mary, in such pain during His crucifixion.

I told Him that I was living in a body that didn't work. I described what it was like to be on a ventilator and not be able to breathe or function with the weakness of a body that didn't work. I told Jesus I wanted to stay in heaven with Him, that this whole experience had taught me to let go of everything and everyone I have loved, and that I was all right with this because I knew I would be with them again.

I began to cry. Jesus asked me to understand that He was asking me to do this because He needed me to explain to others that death is not painful and is not the end.

"It is your decision to make," He said, adding that He would really appreciate my help in getting this message across to others.

I asked Him, "How can You show me all that I have seen during this time with You and then ask me to go back to a body that doesn't work, to the pain and agony I was experiencing once again?"

All of a sudden, He took my face into His hand and looked straight into my soul. He asked me, "Do you love Me?"

I cried, "Lord, You know I love You." Tears were streaming down my cheeks. I was overcome with emotion.

"Will you go back for Me?" He asked.

I replied, "Why would You bring me here and show me everything You have and let me experience this precious love and then ask me to go back?" I shouted, "Do You realize how much pain I was in before You brought me here? Do You realize the body I am functioning in? It doesn't work right!"

He smiled at me and then again asked, "Do you love Me?"

I looked down and then up at Him and said quietly, "Yes, Lord. You know I love You."

He said, "There is much more for you to do for Me. I brought you to this place so that you could experience a taste of what heaven was like, to give you renewed hope, and to give you some idea of what awaits you when you come back. Will you go back and continue My work?" He added, "If you choose to go back and help Me, when you return here, what you have experienced is nothing in comparison to what is waiting for you."

I smiled and then begged Him to show me one of the upper realms, but He said He could not do this because I would never consider going back if He showed me what was waiting for me.

"Will you go back and help Me?" He repeated.

I then said yes.

I walked in heaven alongside of Jesus and saw things I never thought possible. I met souls I somehow affected through my prayers. Jesus then placed both hands on top of my head and sent me back. I could feel myself literally pushed back into my body through my head.

I felt like I had been gone for several days, but in our time, it was only about fifteen minutes. Sister Judy said that once they got the crash team into place and stopped the blood transfusion, my heart rate and breathing became more normal. She said after this, I sat up in the bed, with my hands raised in a prayerful manner and my eyes open, looking upwards. She said the doctors kept coming into the room and tried to get me to respond to stimuli. They kept putting needles in my neck and fingers, without response. Sister Judy finally asked them to just "give her some time and to please stop pinching and poking her with needles."

When I finally opened my eyes, the first person I saw was Sister Judy. I said, "Judy, you won't believe what just happened to me."

She said, "Oh, I'll believe. I saw you."

I described what I had just experienced, and she told me that I had been given a special gift from God.

Over the next several months, I tried to articulate what I learned and the message I was given to spread: **ALL LIFE HAS MEANING.**

In obedience to Jesus, I have shared numerous times over the last nineteen years with anyone who needed or wanted to hear what happened to me.

Everyone I have shared my story with has asked me why I hadn't written a book on this experience. I promised God that I would give it my best in the hope that the message given to me on that day will be read, discussed, and understood more fully by those facing death or having a loved one die.

My Life in Motion Pictures

God wants us to expect the impossible. We try to do the right things while understanding that even if we've made mistakes, gone off course, or not followed the path set by God, we can begin again many times throughout our life. Throughout this entire experience, I have learned that Jesus is with me, now and forever. He will never leave me alone. I know that everything on earth happens for a reason. Although we may not like what happens and question God about it, He directs us at all times. It is possible to find God in pain and illness. It is not easy to live daily with sickness.

People want to know how I was able to accept what was happening to me without bitterness or anger. I didn't want to have this disease. I didn't have time to be sick, I told Him. I was asked to be open to feeling what it is like to live in a body that didn't work. God and His angels were with me through my whole experience. I was asked to walk, one step at a time, while holding Jesus's hand. I was asked to trust Him, and I did. I am forever grateful for this experience.

About a year after all this happened, I became sick once again. I developed numerous gallstones and needed to have my gallbladder removed. Whenever I needed to be operated on, my neurologist needed to clear me for surgery due to my myasthenia gravis. My gallbladder was removed via laparoscopic surgery, and the next day, I was sitting next to my hospital bed when I suddenly had a coughing spell. My wounds started to bleed, and everyone became alarmed.

When I left the hospital about three days later, my abdomen was black and blue. I remember how weak I felt once again. I still had to take Mestinon to help lift my muscles due to the MG, and now the pain of this surgery was really dragging me down.

Upon returning home, I went straight to my own bed, and once my legs and arms were cushioned with pillows, I finally fell asleep. Even though I was in a lot of pain, I decided to not take medication for it; instead, I offered my pain up to God. I remember drifting in and out of sleep and being so exhausted from this hospitalization that I began questioning how this experience could help me do what I was sent back to do.

I fell asleep for about two hours. When I woke up, to my great delight, I saw Jesus holding my hand and sitting right next to my bed.

I asked Him, "What are You doing here?"

He said, "I have something to show you."

I told Him, "I don't understand."

He said, "Watch and understand."

He put His hand up, and right before my eyes, something that resembled an old projector screen appeared before me. I saw myself as a toddler, running and playing in a park. I fell down and was crying; Jesus was right behind me.

He picked me up, comforted me, kissed my leg that was hurt, and sent me off to play again. Then I saw myself around the age of four, bathing my infant of Prague statue. I was powdering Him and dressing Him and then watched myself fall asleep with Him snuggling and looking very comfortable. Jesus showed me that He was there.

I saw myself at around seven years old, being carried home by one of my cousins. I had fallen and had lots of blood coming out of my mouth; right beside me, I saw Jesus once again.

I then saw myself in the chapel at St. Agnes School of Nursing, crying about a patient we had lost; Jesus was right next to me, with His hand on my shoulder.

I remember how emotional I was viewing all of this. I didn't want it to stop but had to go to the bathroom. I told Him, "I'm afraid this is a dream and that when I come back from the bathroom, You'll be gone."

He told me to go and assured me that He would be there when I returned.

After I returned, I got comfortable in my bed, and Jesus continued to show me how throughout my life, He had been with me. He then showed me my father's sudden death at the age of fifty-eight.

I saw myself go from an adult woman to a small toddler throwing a temper tantrum because I wanted my daddy. I saw myself hiding from Jesus because I was angry with Him for taking my father so young. In this video of my memories, Jesus stood out in the middle of our living room with His arms extended, calling me to come to Him; I refused for the longest time. Finally, I saw myself peeking around a couch and then running to Him for comfort. I saw myself sobbing at the loss of my father and being held, reassured, and comforted by Jesus.

After being shown all of the above, Jesus reminded me that I was chosen by Him to do certain things in my life. He assured me that I was a child of God who was given certain gifts and that I needed to be open to using those gifts as I grew closer to Him. When all of this was over, my pain was gone.

The next thing I remembered was hearing Steve coming through the door with a TV table and a computer. I asked him why he was bringing the computer into our bedroom, and he replied, "You need to start writing your book."

I was so weak from the surgery that I really couldn't sit up and type anything. He said that he didn't care if I typed one letter at a time. He thought it would be a great time to start, as I was going to be in bed for another six weeks before I could go back to work.

It took me at least six years to feel better physically; during this time, I was driven to and from many of my consulting contracts by the women and men who worked with my company, Excellence in Caring. God truly blessed me with a great support group of nurses and administrators, who helped me get back to a somewhat normal life. I feel that each of us has made a difference in each other's lives. Life moved on, as I continued to do long-term consulting to improve the quality of life in nursing homes, assisted living centers, and adult medical day care facilities. I never will forget what it was like to live in a body that didn't work.

Here are some of the things I learned:

- I learned to be patient with myself.
- Everything doesn't have to be done today.
- Allow myself time and permission without guilt to rest when needed.
- Create a to-do list and be happy if only one thing is crossed off the list that day.
- Stop being so hard on myself.
- I learned to be centered while in prayer.
- I can't do everything I used to do.
- Become an actor and not a reactor to situations you have no control over.
- God is always there, ready to lead and guide me in all aspects of my life.
- God loves me unconditionally.
- God will never leave me.
- He is my strength and my song.

Hospice

Once I was back to work full-time, I prayed for guidance as to what God wanted me to become involved with. In December 2010, I was contracted to help put together a hospice program. The building the owners wanted to use had been the home of a prominent family. After the property was left to Religious Sisters, it served as a home for girls, a working farm for orphan boys, a retreat house, and a retirement home for elderly Sisters. My company was contracted to set up policies and procedures so this facility could be licensed as a hospice.

Hospice is a holistic care philosophy that focuses on quality of life rather than length of life for patients with advanced illnesses. We stressed a body, mind, and spirit approach. As a team, we tried to control pain with symptom management and supportive therapies so patients felt some control over their lives. Family, friends, caregivers, neighbors, and even pets were invited to participate in the care of their loved ones. The teams consisted of a live-in physician (who was available 24/7); RNs and LPNs; social workers; spiritual counselors; nutritionists; physical, occupational, and speech therapists; hospice aides; and specially trained volunteers who assisted in meeting the needs of our residents. I was the administrator at this facility and worked with a wonderful woman named Jean, who led the efforts on putting the whole place together and getting it opened.

There are a million stories that I could share with you just based on this experience alone. I will forever be grateful for working with these wonderful people. God led me to share my story with so many patients facing death. It was unbelievable, even to me.

One situation I must share involved a hospice patient who was of Cuban descent. He was writhing in pain, as he had cancer throughout his whole body. When he arrived, it was during Easter week. I remember seeing an onslaught of people of all ages come into the hospice with this new admission; I went into our parlor to greet this rather large family. The patient's wife spoke poor English but understood the language when spoken to. His children and grandchildren were all very anxious, and none of them wanted to leave until things were situated. I noticed that the family had stayed through the night talking and praying together, and those grandchildren who left came back early the next morning. His wife stayed there the entire time. When she wasn't next to her husband, she sat in the parlor on a chair looking down to the floor, grieving and praying.

I remember bringing the children games and serving drinks, sandwiches, and snacks, just to make sure no one was going to pass out. I finally sat down next to his wife and noticed she was wearing a bracelet that had the cross, saints, and the Blessed Mother on it.

I introduced myself as the administrator and asked her if she was Catholic, and she said, *"Si."*

I asked her if she would like to go to the chapel to pray, and she stated that she was "forbidden" to go to church by her husband. I asked her why, and she explained that when Castro closed down Cuba, her husband had gotten only half of his family out, and he blamed God for not getting the others out. She explained that ever since that happened, her husband would wake up every day and shake his fist at God, cursing Him for not allowing his family to get out.

Because he hated God for this, he forbade her to attend church the entire time they were married. She said she had prayed for sixty years for his soul to come back to Jesus before he died. She was very fearful that he didn't have much time left but believed fervently that a miracle was going to happen. She stated that the whole time he had been sick, he cursed God for his inability to get well and felt that God cursed him because he shook his fist at Him in hate.

I asked her if I could share my experience with her. I showed her my scar and told her about my disease. I explained that I had my own out-of-body experience, and before I knew it, all thirty family members were sitting with us, listening and translating for those who didn't understand. She cried when I explained to her that her husband needed to ask God to come into his heart, that Jesus won't force himself on anyone. Everyone has a free will, and He respects it.

She then asked me if I would come and share with her husband what I had just told her. With his permission, he allowed me to share my experiences. She interpreted what I said; he cried and said, "God won't forgive me."

I explained to him that God would forgive him; all he had to do was ask. He cried and begged to be forgiven; he told his wife that he would ask Jesus to forgive him. He told her that he wanted to see a priest for Confession and Communion. I knew from looking at his vital signs that he didn't have long to live. I called the social workers and case managers and asked them to find a priest.

Everyone we called reminded our staff that it was Holy Thursday; they were preparing for the washing of the feet ceremony. I spoke to one pastor and told him that I had a patient here who had been away from his faith for over sixty years and had cursed God every day; he now wanted to go to Confession and only had about an hour to live.

The pastor asked, "What do you need?"

I explained that I needed a priest to hear his Confession, serve Communion for about thirty family members and the patient, and lead this family in prayers. He said he would send a priest, who arrived at the facility within ten minutes.

The priest immediately went into the patient's room and heard his Confession; he gathered everyone into the room and offered Holy Communion to this man and his wife, along with every other family member who was there. This was their miracle. He died in his wife's arms, peacefully and without pain, within the hour. The entire family came out praising God and thanking Him for this wonderful miracle. His wife grabbed me and thanked me for helping God answer her prayers. She had prayed for something like this to happen before he died, and she said, "God and the Blessed Mother answered my prayer."

This facility was a blessing in my life. I worked with wonderful professionals who knew there was a spiritual side to death and allowed patients to face their concerns rather than push them aside. That first year, more than three hundred people died at the hospice. They died with dignity, love, and peace. God allowed me the time and position to share with many of those who died, as well as their families, what had happened in my life together with my belief that death is not the end.

We had a barbeque every week in the summer. Family members could use the outdoor pool, planted flowers together, and had weddings and funerals at the hospice. These staff members all believed that life needs to be lived to its fullest and that all things happen for a reason. I do believe that God handpicked those who worked at the hospice to help so many in need.

Before I left the hospice position, one of the neighbors confided in me that she knew how many people had passed away the night before. When I asked her how she knew, she said she had seen spiritual beings on the roof of the hospice (she referred to them as angelic beings), escorting the souls of those who had died to heaven. I am not surprised by this. Many people who died at the hospice were ready. It didn't matter if they were Jewish, Catholic, Christian, agnostic, Buddhist, Muslim, or of any other faith or belief system. It was evident to all involved that this was a holy place.

During my first week at this facility, a family member of one of our residents asked if she could donate flowers and plants. I said absolutely. When I returned that next week, a huge truck had delivered flowers and plants of every kind. I asked who ordered them and learned that the family member owned a commercial flower and plant farm. There were so many beautiful flowers and plants; I wondered how we'd be able to plant them all before they died. That weekend, we were having a Fourth of July BBQ for families and residents. Many visitors who came for the BBQ asked if we needed help planting the flowers and plants. Our response was a resounding yes. We gave each family member a large spoon to dig up the dirt, and before we knew it, all of the flowers and plants that were donated were in the ground.

This process brought many different family members together, and while they planted flowers in honor of the residents, they were heard talking with each other, introducing themselves to each other, and slowly becoming a support for each other. People who entered the hospice said they felt like they were walking into a little piece of heaven because the flowers were so beautiful. The goals of hospice care is for patients and their families to experience what has meaning for each individual. We want them to have control over the time they have left, to live life to its fullest. Hospice care is also for the family members who are dealing with the death of a loved one; it assists with grief and counseling.

Stories of Hope

I have found that hope is an enormously powerful emotional state. Expectation, trust, wishes, optimism, anticipation, and confident desire are potent dimensions of hope. Even when you are overwhelmed or filled with negativity, and it seems like you have no control, you really do. You can choose to be negative and complain all day long. Or you can remain calm and peaceful and offer up your suffering for someone else's needs. At those times, you need to refocus on the hope you have in Christ. Then apply this hope and viewpoint to your stressful situation.

Hope can lift your perspective from weary feet to glorious views of the high road, the road to heaven: way better than ice cream. How do you live your life? What's your daily attitude, the lens you use to view life, your outlook for your future? Do your heart and daily actions display the ultimate hope that lives powerfully in you? Or do you have a tantrum because hope has been sucked from you or seems distant and out of reach?

It is the Spirit of Jesus Who infuses hope into our hearts. When you do focus on this hope, the road ahead is doable whether it's rough or smooth.

One story at this hospice involved a young man who had Down's syndrome. I will call him James. He was about forty years old physically, but emotionally, James was about eight years old. He came to the hospice because he was diagnosed with liver and pancreatic cancer. Every day at the hospice, James would walk up and down the hallway, greeting each resident and their families. He had just moved into a group home and was working his first job when he had received his diagnosis of cancer. Despite this, he had a constant smile on his face and brought great joy to everyone.

James said he was so happy that he was going to die because he was going to be reunited with his mother, who had died several years prior. He claimed that he had a dream whereby Jesus told him that he didn't need to be afraid about dying. Jesus explained to him that dying was going to be like him getting onto an elevator and going up to the top floor; when the doors opened up, he was going to run to his mother's arms. He couldn't wait.

We asked him to tell us what he'd like to do, since he knew he only had a short time to live. He finally told the staff what he always wanted to do but wasn't able to. He wanted to wear a doo rag and helmet and ride on a motorcycle. Well, Jean, the executive director, knew who to call and arranged for him to be surprised the next day. Several motorcycles came to the facility to pick him up. The staff made sure he knew what to do. They gave him his own doo rag and helmet to put on his head, and he rode a motorcycle all around the parking lot. He was so happy.

James was a musician, and that week, his father had invited several of his friends from the group home to bring their instruments over for one last concert. James dedicated this concert to his family for "always taking care of him." He reassured everyone that he wasn't afraid of death because of his dream; he couldn't wait to see his mommy. He died several days later, peacefully and without pain. His family stayed by his side and commented to the staff about "how wonderful he was and how special they felt that God allowed him to be a part of their lives."

Before he died, we spoke about heaven, and I described to him what I experienced. He was so accepting of my story and receptive to the fact that he was going to die and would be with his mother again.

One day, we had five residents dying at the same time: two elderly residents, one man about fifty-six, one young woman around seventeen, and another young mother around thirty years old. The staff worked like a well-oiled machine. I was so proud of all of them.

The pastoral counselors even went to the homes of these residents to retrieve their pets. The two elderly residents each had a large dog. When their pets were brought in, these dogs immediately got onto their beds and snuggled with their owners. Two cats were also brought in to the individual rooms of their owners. One dog did not have his rabies shots up to date, so I called a veterinarian who lived near the facility and asked if he could give the shot, and he came right away to do so. This dog was brought to her owner's room, and once she was up onto the bed, she found a place to snuggle right next to her owner. Staff used pet therapy, music therapy, comfort foods, favorite games, and numerous other things to keep the residents involved and help them accept what was occurring.

It really doesn't matter what faith you are here on earth. I believe that God loves all humankind. His message is for everyone, and He comes to people in all forms. I want to share with you about a man named Isaac. He was dying in the hospital, where I was his primary nurse. I was encouraged to keep him sedated throughout the shift. At that time, I remember we worked twelve-hour shifts.

For two days, I remember watching Isaac's only son go into his room, only to come out with his head hanging low. The tearful look on his face said it all. I approached him to ask if there was anything I could do for him to assist him in the care of his father. He told me that he wanted to speak with his father and pray with him, but each time he came in, he was sedated. So the next time I checked on Isaac, I informed him that his son wanted to speak with him and pray with him. He agreed that it was very important and asked me to hold the morphine so he would be able to pray with his son. I did this at his request.

About six o'clock that evening, Isaac's son came back and saw that his father was more alert and able to talk with him. They spent about two hours speaking with each other, and then the son came out and said that his father wanted to speak with me. When I came to the room, Isaac thanked me profusely for keeping him clear minded so he could speak with his son one more time. I will never forget him. He told me that he was ready to receive the shot now, and I gave it to him.

Once he had the medication, he asked his son and me to join hands with him and to pray. He was Jewish but saw that I was wearing a cross around my neck. He said, "Let's say the Our Father."

We did pray together, and at the end of the prayer, he expired. Both his son and I saw a white wisp of his spirit rise out of his body and leave. He also had a glow about him.

I had not understood the principles of faith regarding Judaism. Before he died, Isaac told me about Jewish principles of faith, which included the following:

- God does exist.
- God is one and unique.
- God is incorporeal.
- God is eternal.
- Prayer is to be directed to God alone and to no other.
- The words of the prophets are true.
- Moses was the greatest of the prophets, and his prophecies are true.
- The Written Torah (first five books of the Bible) and the oral Torah (teachings now contained in the Talmud and other writings) were given to Moses.
- There will be no other Torah.
- God knows the thoughts and deeds of people.
- God will reward the good and punish the wicked.
- The Messiah will come.
- The dead will be resurrected.

As you can see, these are very basic and general principles. Judaism focuses on relationships: the relationship between God and humankind, between God and the Jewish people, between the Jewish people and the land of Israel, and between human beings. The Jewish scriptures tell the story of the development of these relationships, from the time of creation, through the creation of the relationship between God and Abraham, to the creation of the relationship between God and the Jewish people, and forward. The scriptures also specify the mutual obligations created by these relationships, although various movements of Judaism disagree about the nature of these obligations.

Some say they are absolute, unchanging laws from God (Orthodox); some say they are laws from God that change and evolve over time (Conservative); some say that they are guidelines that you can choose to follow or not (Reformed). Isaac felt very ready to die after he had spoken and prayed with his son. He understood that death was not the end, and he wasn't afraid to meet God anymore. He wasn't afraid to die. His wishes were met; he was once again allowed the honor of praying with his son prior to his death. His son stayed with his body until it was picked up. His funeral had to be within twenty-four hours of his death.

My Mother's Death

About ten years ago, my mother died in my home while on hospice. Prior to her death, Mom had congested heart failure, kidney failure, diabetes, hypertension, lung cancer, a fractured hip from a fall, and Alzheimer's disease. She was a character. She knew that she would have the support of all of us when the time came to die. She could no longer live on her own.

I spoke to Mom for about a year about going on hospice. She kept telling me she wasn't ready to do that yet. She loved the Blessed Mother, and so about two months before she died, we started to say the Rosary together daily. Every morning, I would give her a second cup of coffee and discuss who she thought she had to forgive. She would ask me daily why she was still alive. I told her I didn't know but that maybe if we started talking about people she knew in the past that she felt hurt her, she could begin to forgive them. So, every day, she would remember someone who had hurt her or some event she thought she needed to forgive someone about, until it became really hard for her to find anyone else she needed to forgive.

I knew that Mom was failing daily. She was falling more and needed assistance with her bathing, grooming, and walking. She didn't want to go out anymore and much of the time didn't want to get dressed.

She fell at my home one day after she was discharged from a hospital stay, and she broke her right hip. She needed to have an ambulance transport her to the ER, and they operated. It was over the holidays, and the surgeon informed me that she needed a titanium plate to fix her hip; it couldn't be delivered until December 26. She was in severe pain; nothing seemed to help her. At one point, after getting the staff to give her pain medication, she was crying in pain. I decided that I was going to crawl into bed with her and try to rock her into a less painful position.

I lay next to my mother, put my arms around her, and held her. She stopped crying and told me how much she missed human touch. So I spent that night holding her, trying to comfort her, singing to her, and just held her to the best of my ability.

Sometime after the operation, as she was getting ready to be discharged, I went to pick her up and asked if I could see her chart. The chart indicated that she was supposed to have a CAT scan of her lungs, but it had not been done. The physician told me that it could be done as an outpatient.

I said, "Since she's here, let's get it done."

So they took her to the CAT scan for her lungs, and when she came back, the doctor came in and said they had bad news: Mom had a tumor on the left lung that they believed was cancer.

I went out to the desk and saw several physicians I knew and asked them what they would do if it was their mother. They advised me to get a brain scan done to determine if the cancer had spread to that area. We did obtain this scan, and they found no sign of the cancer spreading at that time. Mom then had surgery that took out the cancerous portion of her lung; she didn't want any chemo or radiation. She just wanted to come home.

When she came home, I could tell how exhausted she was. That is when I began to speak to her again about hospice. She was only seventy-six years old.

One day after breakfast, Mom spoke very clearly to me about it; she had decided she wanted to do hospice. She was sick of getting all the medication she was on; she complained that all food tasted metallic because of her insulin injections, and she didn't want any pills or insulin anymore. She stated she wanted to eat whatever she wanted. Once she was on hospice, all of her pills and insulin were taken away.

I told my brothers and sister that Mom only had about three weeks left to live because she was off all her heart medication and insulin.

Mom wanted to go to the casinos in Atlantic City one more time, so my brother Tommy took her for the day. She really enjoyed herself but came back exhausted. She would rally herself when my brothers and sister came to visit. Once she knew they had left, she wanted to go right back into the bed. We found out the cancer had spread to her bones after this. We knew we didn't have much time left with her. We each took turns sitting next to Mom because the one thing she requested was to not die alone. She told her priest that she was ready to go into the next big adventure of her life and was finally going to be with her husband after being separated more than twenty-five years.

Mom and I spoke many times about my out-of-body experience. She wanted to hear my story over and over. She told me she couldn't wait to be with God in heaven. I remember we spent every day doing a life review with her. The night before she died, my brother Tim was sitting next to her in a lounge chair, holding her hand. We were taking turns being with her so she wouldn't die alone. I went to sleep upstairs with Steve, when all of a sudden, I felt someone staring at me; it was Tim.

He explained that he was really upset because Mom was having a conversation with her guardian angel. He stated that she even introduced the angel to him. I went downstairs to sleep next to my mother and hold her hand. She had another conversation with her guardian angel and tried to introduce me to him. Then she had a glow to her face. She claimed she saw the Blessed Mother. She said she was a small woman, dressed in white with a blue sash, who came to tell her that she would be with God in heaven soon.

Mom prayed every day that my father would come to get her when it was time for her to die. About one hour later, I smelled Old Spice. This was the cologne my father used to wear (there was none in my home). Then I saw my mother with a glow about her face, and she informed me that "Daddy was here." She asked me if I saw him. I told her I smelled his cologne, and she smiled. She described him to me. She said he had on his white captain's uniform with gloves and hat.

He told her that he would be taking her soon and that they would be together in heaven. She said he looked like he was twenty-eight years old again, so young.

Toward the end of Mom's life, I spoke to the Little Servant Sisters of the Immaculate Conception from St. Joseph's Senior Home, who were praying for my mother. They suggested that I gently open a window or door, "so that her spirit could go." I ever so gently opened sliding glass doors about a quarter of an inch. They had curtains on them, and there was no wind that day to indicate that the door was slightly opened. When Mom woke up from her nap, she asked me to close the door. I asked her how she knew the door was open, as it had curtains in front of it. She explained to me that "they are all calling to me; they want me to go with them, but I am not ready yet. I need to wait for Tommy to get off his ship and come here."

I called everyone I knew that next day and told them if they wanted to see Mom, they needed to come immediately, as she wouldn't be around much longer. I must have had at least twenty people come into my home that night. One of my cousins brought Italian pastries, and Mom loved it. We all began to speak about Mom and recalled various times she had helped everyone during her lifetime; many stories were shared. The room was full of laughter, and my mother began to clear her throat. I thought she might be in pain, but when I asked her if she needed anything, everyone became quiet.

She joked, "I'm dying over here," and added, with a loving smile, that she felt like she was attending her own wake. Lying there listening to the many funny stories and experiences she had with each of us made her realize how loved she really was.

She said she only had one more thing to do, and then she could go. She was waiting for my oldest brother, Tommy, to come. She took time to speak with each one of us individually about our lives and how much she appreciated having us as children and how grateful she was to us for helping her throughout her life. That morning, when Tommy finally arrived, she was struggling to breathe. I knew her heart, lungs, and body were full of fluid, and her urine bag was empty. All four of us were ready. We lifted her head up to help position her better, as she was struggling to breathe; all of a sudden, she was gone. Every line in her face relaxed, and she had a beautiful glow about her that told us she was with God.

My sister Susan said, "Look at her face."

Mom looked fifty years younger; no more pain, only peace. Most people who are dying don't want to die alone and turn to some faith to help deal with their death. The beauty of this action is that deep down inside of the human being is a soul that seeks to be transformed and to be free.

God Honors Your Will

Whenever people hear about death and God, they ask why things are the way they are on earth. The answer is because God waits for us to open the door for Him to enter our lives. He wants you to open the door to His love. I realize that life is never going to be perfect.

I was told that we're all here for a particular reason. Jesus sent us here to do what we're supposed to do. We have to be open to what God desires for us so that our lives evolve according to His purpose. Death is just the next step in our spiritual journey. It's not an end, but a beginning, and when we view it like that, we can make choices while we are living to help make our deaths easier.

Everything I do, I pray about. Jesus is my life, my love, and my destiny. God wants all of humanity to understand that you do not have to be afraid when it's time to die. Death is the next step in your spiritual journey. Death is not the end; it is the beginning. It is coming home, reconnecting with all of your family and friends as well as spiritual people you have assisted by praying for them. We need to especially pray for those who have no one left to pray for them here on earth.

There are events in our past that are life-changing:

- career choices
- getting married
- having children
- moving
- sudden death or illness

- job loss
- divorce

Each of the above can completely knock us off the course we thought our lives were taking. I know that my initial reaction to my illness was denial; I told my neurologist that he was ridiculous for even suggesting I was so ill. Every experience is an opportunity to dig deeply within ourselves and find out things that we would not have realized if not for this life-changing experience. With each situation listed above, you can either throw in the towel or roll with the punches.

I have learned much from my life journey. I know for a fact that Jesus will carry me through any and every event I am faced with, whether it is good or bad. I have learned that no one really understands what you're going through, unless they've experienced it themselves. I now know what it's like to be living in a body that doesn't work.

People don't always show signs of chronic pain. Someone once shared with me that the key to coping with pain is to control your pain instead of letting your pain control you. When I accepted the fact that my pain was here to stay, then I allowed it to feel familiar, to become a part of my daily life. I learned to modify my schedule to allow extra time for tasks, which are more difficult now. I listen to my body more. When I am tired, I rest or take a nap. I give myself permission to relax. I have also learned to worry productively. Someone once shared with me that it's a good idea to take about fifteen minutes a day to concentrate on whatever it was you're worried about.

At times, when certain problems come up over and over again, I write about them in my journal to assist me while thinking them through. Whatever pain I do have brings me directly to God. All of my pain is offered up as redemptive suffering and is united to the sufferings of Jesus.

Chronic pain, like the pain in my muscles, has a way of defining life's true pleasures. I now find more time for myself every single day. I surround myself with my favorite things and with those I love who make me the happiest. I enjoy my grandchildren and friends who understand my illness and limits; these people aren't afraid to laugh with me. Even though there have been times when I felt that God was so far away and not hearing my cries, I know deep within that He was right there next to me.

Something to remember in facing the most challenging experiences of your life: It is not cowardly to seek help from God. He extends healing and forgiveness. Forgiveness is an action word, suggesting a release. It is soothing and healing, reuniting those once torn apart. Forgiveness is an acceptance of the humanity in both parties. I didn't always understand that quiet prayer does not always require a response by God. I realize that my life needs to be passionate regarding using the gifts I've been given. I don't want God to think that I'm unappreciative.

I understand now that when you are dealing with an illness such as myasthenia gravis, you can become consumed by it. Emotions and feelings affect decisions, but spiritual practices can help in healing. God is the author of compassion and engages in the spirit of healing. You must find strength and God's light within so that you can calm the spirit and heal the soul.

God is such a great comforter. Jesus taught me that even when I am hurting, I should turn to Him and pray for others with compassion. He said it is all right to hold someone's hand and cry together, to show compassion for others. Compassion is caring in action. It is the way of Jesus to help one hurting person at a time.

Making a Difference in the Lives of Others

You can make a difference in the lives of other people by showing empathy, love, and encouragement; by listening carefully; by understanding; and by appreciating our differences. I've decided that I won't waste my life on petty things that occur every day. I will be happier without worrying about tomorrow. Today is my time to do God's work, in the present moment. God introduces us to people for a reason. People come into and go from our lives for various reasons.

They may be sent to lift you up when you're feeling down. They may be sent to teach a life lesson. Do you ever wonder why someone calls out of the blue when you need someone to talk with about a situation? That is God sending someone to assist you. I remember reading somewhere that "people come into our lives and go. Others stay for a while, leave footprints on our hearts, and we are never, ever the same." I have been so blessed by the people God has sent into my life. I am also forever grateful for the opportunity to help God and others in any way possible.

I have learned throughout my life that God has many gifts for each of us. All we need to do is ask. I am not shy about asking Him for the many gifts He wants to give me; I now know that all of His gifts will make me better able to follow His lead. I have the ability to speak in front of others, the gift of passion for what I believe regarding what happened to me, and a fearlessness in sharing my wonderful experience. These gifts have helped many people die with less fear and more understanding about what was about to happen.

Too often, we live our lives as if we have an unlimited time with our families and friends. Without warning, God took my father at the age of fifty-eight, and my life was turned upside-down. I wished I had spoken to him one more time. I remember kissing him goodbye but never realized it would be the last time I saw him alive. I have learned that the time we have here on earth is limited. I don't want to look back on my life with regrets that I didn't tell someone I loved them or cherished their friendship. Every day, we are given the opportunity to embrace the special moments we are given by God. We need to make whatever time we have with those we love count.

We should not wait to tell our loved ones how we feel or how much they are loved. Everyone should live their lives authentically. This doesn't mean we won't make mistakes. We all meet challenges in parenting and relationships along the way. Sometimes, these challenges make us want to scream or cry.

We may allow a situation to immobilize us and give us self-doubt. When I was in a wheelchair after surgery for my myasthenia gravis, I realized that even though someone looks all right on the outside, it doesn't mean they are physically okay on the inside. I remember being wheeled by my husband and children while in Florida shortly after one of my surgeries, and people would look at me and say loudly, "What's wrong with her?"

Small acts of kindness and understanding go a long way. Kindness eases another's burdens. A gentle hug, a card with prayers, a simple phone call just to say hello may help someone who is in pain or dealing with chronic illness.

What we fail to realize is that we are surrounded with hurting people. Some wear masks to hide their scars, not wanting anyone else to know how much they are hurt. When someone is hurting, it is very important to be available in action, not just in comments. They need to feel safe, to disclose the pain they are experiencing. They need to know that what they share won't be brushed off or become a joke. We need to offer a shoulder to cry on when they are feeling so alone. We need to be present but not too pushy.

We need to take the lead from the person who needs the hug. No matter how strong someone comes across, when they are involved in a major life change, we need to realize that no one is born super-human. Nothing insulates a person from the pain of the moment. After all we had been through, Steve and I decided a long time ago to embrace all major life changes as an opportunity to live through them and gain wisdom through our response to them.

I think of all the types of people Jesus connected with while on earth: murderers, prostitutes, tax collectors, those who were paralyzed, marginalized, and possessed. All the people He touched were really down to their last thread, hanging on for dear life. Jesus came into their lives and brought hope. He told them that they shouldn't give up. They needed to anchor themselves in Him.

God created us to be fully human. He made us. Each of us are a somebody. God has given us gifts; we should use them wisely. We want to be ourselves, make mistakes, and then ask God for forgiveness. If we messed up, it's not the end of the world. We are called to be responsible and not reckless. God encourages us to open our eyes, admit our blunders, apologize, fix the problem, and avoid a repeat performance. Being wrong has taught me humility, and in the process, it has released me from the illusion of perfection. Having the courage to say, "I was wrong," shows strength and character. None of us are flawless. We all make mistakes; we are human. God can forgive anything.

I encourage you to make today the most important day of your life. It is easy to waste time worrying about petty things. If you wander into yesterday and worry about tomorrow, you're passing up the only time you really have, which is today. Live today now. It is disappearing quickly and will never come again. Enjoy the journey. Remember that people walk into your life for a reason. They may be there to lift you up, teach you a life lesson, hear you speak, or help you decide what to do next.

When you are faced with death and don't have much time to repair family relationships, you need to get your life in order or communicate better with those you love. You need to ask God to help you do what's necessary. There is a still, small voice deep within each person that gets louder when they are being urged to do something. Many are afraid of looking like a fool. I am not afraid of looking like a fool to anyone. I follow God's lead whenever I open up and speak to people about my experiences. God is so good.

Death is a part of life that most people refuse to deal with ahead of time. Some of us are given the gift of knowing how much time we have left. We are given the opportunity of tying up loose ends, saying goodbye, healing wounds with relatives and friends. I think I would want this to happen to me so I could be ready, willing, and able to move on to the next big spiritual adventure of my life. I do not believe that death is the end, but the beginning. I have been blessed with a unique experience involving death. This book is a way to share my experience with others in a hope that death will be seen as a sacred journey to a fuller life with Jesus.

Sacred Journey

After writing this book, I realize now how the sudden death of my cousins, their grandfather's suicide, and the many tragic deaths of public figures trapped me for a long while. I believe that I needed to face my fears of dealing with death and dying, by working through it in my nursing profession and finally being open to allowing myself to go through a daily walk with Jesus, letting all this baggage go.

I was in a form of crisis when I was told I had myasthenia gravis. I feared loss of control, loss of self-image, and loss of independence. I was afraid of abandonment by family and friends, of isolation from others because of my limitations. As you know, we are often judged in this world by the things we accomplish. We rate our success on how much we do rather than on who we are as individuals.

Healing means being able to live life to the fullest capacity possible, regardless of the circumstances. Everything is intertwined. This process takes patience, prayer, and the support of family and friends, as well as guidance from the medical and spiritual community. All of this does help. Every day, my life experience has taught me that life is hard. Problems will always be there. Medical issues, financial issues, and whatever it takes to survive will one day be knocking at every person's door.

I have experienced absolute lack of control where my body is concerned. My muscles drop when I am too stressed or in any sort of dangerous position; even when I am walking outside to try to get some fresh air, the heat can affect my muscles. Some days, I would create a to-do list and find myself crossing one item out of ten listed because

I did not have the physical energy or muscle strength to do the other nine items. I had to give myself permission to not feel guilty.

My relationship with God really helped me put things into perspective. Every day when I get up, before my feet even hit the floor, I ask God to help me this day. I pray to receive any and all gifts He wishes to give to me and tell Him I am open to whatever He wants to happen.

I know what my plan is, what I have on my list, but I am open to whatever God wants me to do. When I feel God is distant or not answering my prayer, I experience a void in my life. I continue to pray even though I don't feel His presence or am not getting anything back. Quietly waiting for God's answer to my prayers is one of the hardest things to do, and yet this is the time to believe the most, the time of deepest faith.

God answers our prayers in His time, not our time. Sometimes, things appear so overwhelming that it feels like you really can't catch your breath. This is the time to hunker down and praise God even more. Thank Him for the opportunity to serve Him one more day. I ask God to surround me with His angels in every situation. I ask Him to use me as an instrument of His love to help me serve His people.

I ask God daily to open up my heart, to not judge anyone but to put one foot in front of the other and to guide me in all relationships. Sometimes, I do this routinely, but other times, I fail. And again, it is all right to fail, as long as you continue to try to answer God's call. God teaches us through every situation. Rev. Henri Nouwen's expression called "patient waiting" shows the value of waiting. This kind of waiting is not a passive activity. Patient waiting involves suffering through the present, really entering into what is going on, all the while waiting for God's presence to be manifested in the experience.

As humans, we tend to put things off. We plan to do them when our schedules open up. We need to realize that the time to do the things we want is today because tomorrow may never come. I tell my husband, children, and grandchildren that I love them every day. I want them to feel my love constantly. I remember during my weakest time while hospitalized in an isolation room, I told Steve and our sons that if I was unable to speak, I would squeeze their hands three times to mean "I love you." We used this method when I was on the ventilator, and to this day, we use it when we walk in a room and others are present.

I hug my family a lot; I kiss them every time I see them. I pray with them whenever I get the chance; my prayer for them is that one day, they will experience a very close relationship with God on their own. Steve helps me put things into perspective. He has spoken to me many times about my desire to be with Jesus. I have explained to him that Jesus gave us to each other here on earth, but when we get to heaven, there should be no doubt in either of our spirits that Jesus is Lord. He is not in competition with Jesus. We joke about the fact that there will be no competition; hands down, Jesus has my entire being. I have been blessed with such a wonderful Christian husband who is full of wisdom, understanding, and compassion, who has loved me through sickness and in health. We are one of those "until death do us part" couples.

Our vows have always been sacred to us; God has always been a large part of our relationship. Once when I felt things looked so bleak and thought I would never recover from my myasthenia gravis and was struggling to breathe, I remember telling Steve that he would have to find someone else to marry, as I was going to die. I cried telling him this. The look on his face told me how upset he was. He always loves me unconditionally. I remember he held me in his arms and cried with me and then said that he was not giving up, that God was going to change things for us. He said that we were here for each other in sickness and in health, and no one was dying, as far as he was concerned.

I was very low, as you can imagine. In fact, I was ready to give up the struggle. I didn't see any light at the end of the tunnel. So what did God do? He sent in my Stevie Wonder, and he rescued me from my anguish and despair that day. We prayed together and decided that we were both in this for the long haul. I really didn't think I was going to survive.

My experience taught me that I need to value every encounter while here on earth. My job is to make sure that whoever reads this book realizes that having hope is the same as having Jesus, for He is our hope. Hope seeks the good in all people and reminds us that God is still in control, even in the worst of times. Hope seeks light in darkness.

When I was first diagnosed with myasthenia gravis, I dug in my heels and refused to budge. I was in deep denial and told God that I would not accept this (I tend to tell Him what I think is best for me). But thank God, we have such a close relationship that after allowing me to yell and scream, Jesus gently informed me that I needed to have this experience in order to do His will in the future. He also told me that He would be with me through it all.

I have tried to explain my personal relationship with Jesus. He wants us to be personal with everyone. He wants us to understand that He has walked next to us in every moment of our lives. Even though I have not felt worthy to be accompanied by Jesus, He still was there.

We are created in God's image and likeness. God reminds us that we are called to be happy forever in His love. We are beloved children of God. We need to take ownership of this identity. God loves us just as we are, in this very moment. No one is insignificant. Pope Francis said, "In His eyes, you are precious, and your value is inestimable."

God is always faithful. He loves us even when we fail to love ourselves. He forgives all sins. Don't let any shame hold you back from His forgiveness. Jesus looks beyond our faults and sees the person. He sees future good. He looks into your heart and soul. Jesus is calling you by name.

Encounter Jesus in everyone: the hungry, thirsty, naked, sick, a friend in trouble, a prisoner, the refugee and the migrant, and our neighbors who feel abandoned. God breaks down all fences. He comes to break open everything that we hold hardened in our hearts.

Let it happen.

Printed in the United States
By Bookmasters